LONE STAR CHEFS

bright sky press
HOUSTON, TEXAS

2365 Rice Boulevard, Suite 202,
Houston, Texas 77005

10 9 8 7 6 5 4 3 2 1

Library of Congress Cataloging-in-Publication Data on file with publisher.
ISBN 978-1-933979-80-9

Creative Direction, Ellen Cregan; Photography, Julie Soefer; Design, Wyn Bomar; Cover design, Marla Garcia
Printed in China through RR Donnelley

Texas Masters Share Their Culinary Creations

LONE STAR CHEFS

John DeMers ★ Photography by Julie Soefer

bright sky press

HOUSTON, TEXAS

contents

SO EXACTLY WHAT *IS* A LONE STAR CHEF?

Like every other aspect of the Lone Star State, any answer worth giving to that question is likely to come as a surprise. And this being Texas, I mean a BIG surprise.

When we started this project, this journey, we held in our minds only big, bold statements about the nature of Texas life—ridiculous clichés, in other words. A Lone Star Chef would hail from some tiny town the highway gave up on decades ago, the kind of town I invariably refer to as Hookie Dookie Springs. He would (for in this cliché he probably wouldn't *be* a she) wear large boots and an even larger cowboy hat; talk with a broad, impenetrable Texas drawl; and whenever the going got tough, charm everybody in the kitchen or dining room to pieces with a grin halfway to Dallas. That's, of course, if he wasn't in Dallas already.

What we found, though—and what we *always* find here in Texas—is that for all the talk of things being bigger, one size never fits all. And one vision doesn't either. There are chefs pretty much like that cliché, and others who borrow some attributes without buying into the whole package, and still others who only put it on like a costume when it's time to step onstage. Being a Lone Star Chef is a role, truly, as much as being a New York stockbroker, a Chicago ward politician, or a California surfer. But as we learn every time we watch a play or a movie, there's more than one way to play any role.

To understand the chefs in this book, to join us in sharing their stories and their remarkably inventive recipes, you need to hold two concepts side-by-side in your head. A Lone Star Chef is some once-only, mysterious combination of who you are and what you cook. It is my job in these pages to present you with as much of both as I possibly can.

Some chefs included here actually *do* come from Texas. Stephan Pyles of Dallas, for instance, came from as close to Hookie Dookie Springs as I can imagine, working almost from birth at his parents' truck stop in preparation for one of our state's most illustrious culinary careers. Other chefs, as that bumper sticker puts it, got here as quick as they could. Robert Del Grande of RDG in Houston came from San Francisco, Tom Rapp and Toshi Sakihara in Marfa came from New York (Toshi originally from Okinawa, which isn't anywhere close to Hookie Dookie Springs), and Kent Rathbun came from Kansas City. That we let Kent in *at all* is a testament to our sense of fair play, since he grew up smoking meats in one of the few other places in America that dares to say they know how to make barbecue.

Each chef has a place to be from, each chef has a road that he (or yes, she) traveled to get here, and each chef has created a business based in Texas that expresses, ultimately, anything and everything worth knowing. Food, after all, isn't just a thing on a plate, no matter how glorious that thing or that plate might be. Food is a story of people the chef has loved—mothers and grandmothers most often, but also mentors in the profession—mixed

with books the chef has read, places the chef has been, and ingredients the chef has tasted. This is all on a timeline, starting then and passing through now, a meandering but no doubt caloric journey to someday. On this earth, some people write their autobiographies, but the chefs in this book don't have to. Their life stories are stashed, ready for our ravenous unraveling, beneath every sauce, around the edges of every presentation, and most of all, in the smiles we wear when we connect to them by way of the incredible dishes they set before us.

There was a time—and I, like most of the chefs in this book, am old enough to remember it—when chefs weren't the rock stars, the celebs, the demigods, or even the *artists* so many in the public consider them to be today. They were the worker bees of foodservice, and they were paid accordingly. They were not today's 18-year-olds who throw a bundle of Dad's money at the Culinary Institute of America and expect to step off the stage with their diplomas into the embrace of an agent with TV, cookbook, and endorsement deals for signing. If I can make one solitary generalization that covers all the chefs in this book, it's that they are *not that guy.* Sure, they want to laugh at that guy—they've usually hired him more than a few times, with different faces— but mostly they just want to punch him out. That guy represents everything about the profession that's broadly believed by the public but isn't actually true, everything that sidesteps the hard work and accompanying hard knocks that represent every real chef's education.

I like, love, quibble with, yell at, curse out, respect, and admire the men and women profiled in this book, and I continue to be fascinated by the stories they write anew each time they wake up in the morning. They are dreamers, they are planners, they are laborers, they are artists, all these things and more, depending on which day of the week you catch them and what just happened with their meat guy, their fish guy, their vegetable guy, or their endless parade of wine guys. And heaven forbid you meet them on a day their dishwasher just called in sick. Some days being a Lone Star Chef really is enough to drive you to drink, and at least some of the insights hidden away in these pages were communicated after service late at night when neither the chef nor this humble chronicler was exactly what you might call sober.

So it goes, when you step through those swinging doors. Another world awaits you then, as soon as you turn this introductory page, one that serves up grit and grime in pursuit of pomp and circumstance. If the dining room on one side of those doors is all about fantasy—yours, mine, and ours—the world on the other side is one hard-edged, ice-cold, bracing blast of reality. I like to say a restaurant kitchen is equal parts muscle and magic. Hailing from different places, with different personalities, different cooking styles, and very different lives, these Lone Star Chefs have managed to become masters of both.

rdg + bar annie

rdg + bar annie

▼▼▼▼▼▼▼▼▼▼▼▼▼▼▼▼▼▼▼▼▼▼▼

MORE THAN THREE DECADES INTO THE WACKY SCIENCE EXPERIMENT KNOWN AS COOKING, there is no scientist more excited about his next set of test results than Robert Del Grande. Long of the Houston landmark Café Annie and recently of a signature set of concepts he gathers under his three initials, Robert seldom bothers to mention a dish he created in 1979 or 1993—especially since he's already moved on from a dish he created last week. He will, however, exude boyishly over the food idea he wants to check out tomorrow.

Robert holds a Ph.D. in biochemistry, a fact that some over his long years of cooking have found ridiculous and others perfectly logical. Whatever your reaction, he remains an unlikely collision of personalities and skill sets—those of a clinical researcher and those of a creative artist. The result today is a vision equally unlikely— a tall aging rock star who's still sexy and stylish, covering up a ten-year-old country boy with a cowlick who just got his first chemistry set from the Sears catalogue.

"I was always attracted to science based on asking one question, 'How do things work?'" Robert explains, sitting at a table in the multi-part creation he calls RDG + Bar Annie. "In the mystery and magic out there, there was order to the universe. I was fascinated by how things work, and by how people over the centuries have figured so much of it out. The lure was, and still is, that sense of magic."

Robert's career choice may strike many as unusual, but his endless passion for food and wine should not. He grew up in an Italian family in San Francisco, to him not so much a great restaurant town as a place where relatives always had a delicious meal on the stove. Robert now says he took his mother's terrific cooking for granted; it was simply part of the Italian family landscape. But it formed the man he became. He still believes in sitting down for a meal with those you love, and he still goes pleasurably crazy whenever a new taste opens his eyes to fresh possibilities.

"There was, especially at my grandparents on Sundays, that sense of ceremony," he recalls. "So you think that's the way it always is. My father's parents came from Italy in the early 1900s, so all that culture of food and family was still very much alive for us. My father used to say, 'Go do whatever you want, but be home before dinner.' My mother was a good cook. And she always told me, 'I knew the meal was good because you were humming.'"

Almost before he knew it, Robert's humming and unabashed curiosity about what went on in his mother's kitchen—what *made* the magic—lured him into making the family's breakfast. And when he left home for college, he prepared full meals and set the table, even when he was dining in a spartan apartment by himself. Graduate school produced a couple of roommates who took turns cooking, but Robert's meals remained a treat beyond anything his buddies could pull off. "I brought the food to the table: this wasn't a cafeteria!" he says. Then, with extreme understatement, he adds: "I guess I had a little experience with food being more than taking your hunger away."

"I was fascinated by how things work, and by how people over the centuries have figured so much of it out. The lure was, and still is, that sense of magic."

It was during this period that Robert got his first dishwashing job, not in a restaurant but in a laboratory. And even as he felt his interests tipping gradually away from biology to the more abstract realm of chemistry, he felt his entire life do much the same when he met the cute librarian at the university's science library.

As it turned out, Mimi Kinsman would soon move away from California to the uncharted territory of Houston, Texas, accompanying her sister Candice. And before long, Candice and her husband, Lonnie Schiller, would open a restaurant they called Café Annie. After years of intense scientific pursuit, Robert figured a few months helping out in some kitchen far off in the Lone Star State wouldn't be too hard. And it would keep him close to Mimi.

"I thought it would be fun," Robert says simply. "It was supposed to be three months. And all of a sudden, it was 30 years."

As the history of American restaurants now records, the spirited quartet that formed around Café Annie would become the Schiller Del Grande Restaurant Group, who over the decades gave the world not only one of its best-known New Southwestern destination restaurants but the multi-unit Café Express (sold to Wendy's to add more locations and then purchased back again), the beach-themed Mexican concept Taco Milagro, and the soaring Grove in Houston's downtown park Discovery Green. Schiller Del Grande would do much to enhance Texas dining over those 30 years that caught Robert entirely by surprise—in terms of flavor, in terms of design, in terms of guest experience. And Robert would seem, on any given day, just another regular guy going to work in a business he enjoyed.

Nothing if not analytical, Robert attributes all this success to a series of societal sea changes—things he considers much larger than himself or anything he was ever likely to cook. Beginning in the '60s with Julia Child and continuing with the celebrity chef cookbooks of the '70s and '80s, the American public's hunger for food ideas and a bit of food worship (driven over the top by beautiful color photos) turned insatiable. Chefs and what they did became part of the national conversation in a way no one could have predicted. And home cooks, long satisfied with green bean casserole, set their sights on rack of lamb or even foie gras torchons. And they had the color photos to show them how it was supposed to look, every step of the way.

Linked to this chef-cookbook revolution was the sudden explosion of wonderful new ingredients from around the world, producing increased awareness and sophistication about food, along with fresh herbs where only the dried used to be, and America's strange new love affair with wine. The fact that this love affair was fueled by Robert's home state of California meant that he understood what it meant before many of his

Nothing if not analytical, Robert attributes all this success to a series of societal sea changes.

Texas peers, who were still looking no further than beer or the quasi-official state drink, Crown and Coke. Finally, in a development considered even less likely, Texas discovered a high-end cuisine of its very own.

It was the 1980s and, again with California as their model, region after region across America was exploring its local ingredients and cooking traditions. Suddenly the goal wasn't to serve just a decent duck *a l'orange* but to serve what your grandmother served, and if at all possible, to make it with the fresh, local, seasonal, and sometimes (by default) organic ingredients your grandmother used. It was no big deal, in some ways, Robert insists today. In other ways, it changed everything that food is or can ever mean.

"New Southwestern was fairly simple," he says, hoping to make it sound fairly simple. "It was based on two thoughts. First, to really excel at something, you'd want to be in a position to judge it best yourself. Followed by: what could you be the best judge of? That would be American food, something that would mirror your place and your time."

Within a year or two of serving his first taco, enchilada, or quesadilla, no doubt filled with lobster and/or drizzled with truffle oil, Robert and a handful of other now-iconic Texas chefs had shifted the focus away from all things French to their personal vision of all things Texas. Long-dismissed Mexican flavors (dismissed by European chefs anyway) stood suddenly on equal footing with the French mother sauces, and there rose up an entire obsession with what a combination of fresh, dried, or smoked chile peppers would do to just about any dish.

For many, and probably most, American chefs, creating one restaurant honored with every conceivable award would be plenty for a lifetime. Yet over the years, even as Café Annie grew in prominence, Robert felt his interests drifting toward other ways of cooking, and especially toward other ways of serving. What the industry

dubbed "casualization," a buzzword for the slow death of fancy, formal "fine dining" in America, inspired him to turn his favorite flavors (and especially the multi-cultural mélange his cooks tossed together for themselves at the end of a shift) into Café Express. His intense, and totally ahead of the curve, interest in regional Mexican cuisine—with extra color, extra fun, and extra margaritas added—led him to create Taco Milagro. And by the time the city fathers of Houston were planning Discovery Green, they were simply looking for the best restaurant operators anywhere. They didn't have to look far.

During the summer of 2009, the upscale commercial center long home to Café Annie was shut down for redevelopment. As usual, it was a moment many would find devastating—or a great excuse to take the money and run. To Robert and his trio of interwoven partners, it was an excuse to rethink everything—and to change everything they'd ever secretly wished they could change about Café Annie.

In recent years, it turns out, Robert had regularly found himself pondering the extreme changes in how his guests communicate with each other, how they decide where to eat, and ultimately how they live their business and personal lives. Reservations for special-occasion meals months in advance, he knew, had dried up; his dining room was now packed with people who decided ten minutes earlier on cell phones, or via social networking systems like Facebook and Twitter, where they'd meet for a quick bite. This wasn't your mother's casualization anymore. It was a profoundly different role for a restaurant, as well as for anybody who owns one. And nobody in the whole state of Texas wants to miss a paradigm shift, or wants to be a beloved dinosaur, *less* than that little boy with the cowlick and the chemistry set.

"It has to be true," he says, telling but also asking, as though setting up a science experiment, "that if we change the way we communicate, then we change the way we socialize. And that has to change the way we eat." He stops for a moment, digging around for one of Faulkner's "eternal verities" against a backdrop of traumatic social change. "Still, the Big Question remains: Can you create a dish that, if you have it, you know exactly where you are?"

Thanks to Robert Del Grande, to everything he cooked yesterday and everything he's going to cook tomorrow, the answer to the Big Question is now undeniably Yes.

"It has to be true, that if we change the way we communicate, then we change the way we socialize. And that has to change the way we eat."

By the time the city fathers of Houston were planning Discovery Green, they were simply looking for the best restaurant operators anywhere.
They didn't have to look far.

SEA SCALLOPS ROASTED IN GREEN CORN HUSKS WITH FRESH CORN MAYONNAISE

2   ears fresh corn
3   tablespoons butter, divided
¼   cup mayonnaise
1   tablespoon extra-virgin olive oil
1   teaspoon fresh lime juice
¼   teaspoon salt
1   tablespoon crème fraîche
1   tablespoon grated Cotija cheese
8   large (U-10) sea scallops
Crushed red pepper

Shuck the ears of corn and reserve some of the nicer long corn husks to wrap the scallops. On a box grater over a bowl, grate the ears of corn to produce a course puree. In a small skillet over medium heat, melt one tablespoon butter until foaming. Add the grated corn and stir until thick and creamy. The mixture should resemble soft scrambled eggs. Cool the mixture.

Combine the mayonnaise, olive oil, lime juice, and salt in a mixing bowl, and whip until smooth. Stir in the sautéed corn puree until smooth. Add the crème fraîche and Cotija cheese, and stir to blend. Trim the fresh corn husks lengthwise to the approximate width of a sea scallop. As tight as possible, wrap each sea scallop with the corn husk and secure with a wooden skewer or toothpick.

In a skillet large enough to spaciously hold the sea scallops, melt the remaining two tablespoons of butter over medium heat and gently sauté the scallops until golden brown. Finish cooking the scallops until heated through but not overcooked. Remove from heat. Transfer the sea scallops to serving plates. Spoon some of the fresh corn mayonnaise over each scallop. Very lightly sprinkle with the red pepper flakes. Serves 4.

2 *poblano chiles*
2 *avocados*
4 *ounces queso fresco or aged dry goat cheese*
1 *bunch young purslane, mache, or watercress*
1 *serrano chile, very thinly sliced (optional)*
3 *tablespoons extra-virgin olive oil*
1 *tablespoon fresh squeezed lime juice*
1 *pinch salt and pepper*

Lightly oil the poblano chiles. Over an open gas flame or under a hot broiler, char the skins of the chiles. Allow to cool. Peel the charred chiles. Remove the stems and the seeds. Cut the chiles into small strips.

Cut the avocados in half. Remove the seeds and peel. Cut the avocado halves into thin slices. Cut the queso fresco or goat cheese into small pieces. Remove the stem of the serrano chile, and very thinly slice the chile (optional). Combine the chiles, avocado slices, cheese, and purslane in a mixing bowl. Add the olive oil, lime juice, and a pinch of salt and pepper. Toss lightly. Portion the salad onto dinner plates and serve. Drizzle with a little extra olive oil. Serves 4.

AVOCADO & QUESO FRESCO RELISH:

1   Haas avocado, peeled, seeded, and cut into ½-inch dice
2   ounces queso fresco, cut into ¼-inch cubes
½   serrano chile, very thinly sliced in rounds
¼   white onion, finely chopped
¼   cup cilantro leaves, chopped
1   tablespoon extra-virgin olive oil
1   teaspoon fresh lime juice
½   teaspoon freshly ground black pepper

4   Gulf snapper fillets, about 6 ounces each, skin on
Salt and pepper
1   tablespoon olive oil
Cilantro sprigs

GARLIC-LIME BUTTER:

4   cloves garlic, peeled
1   teaspoon fresh lime juice
1   pinch salt
1   pinch black pepper
1   pinch crushed red pepper
4   tablespoons (½ stick) cold butter

In a small mixing bowl, combine all of the ingredients for the avocado relish. Gently toss or stir with a spoon to mix evenly. Press a piece of plastic wrap on the surface of the relish and refrigerate.

Place the garlic cloves in a small pan and cover with water. Bring the water to a simmer and cook the garlic cloves until they are very soft. Pour off and discard the water. Lightly mash the garlic cloves. Stir in the remaining garlic butter ingredients except for the butter. Set aside.

Lightly salt and pepper the fish fillets. Over medium-high heat, heat the oil in a broad nonstick skillet large enough to comfortably hold the fillets. Sear the skin side of the fillets until light brown and crisp. Turn the fillets over and lower the heat. Gently finish cooking the fillets. When the fish is ready, add the butter to the pan with the mashed garlic mixture. Heat the pan until the butter melts and just begins to foam. Remove from the heat immediately.

Transfer the fillets to dinner plates. Spoon some of the avocado relish over each fillet. Spoon the garlic-lime butter over the fillets. Garnish with cilantro sprigs and serve. Serves 4.

2   pounds country-style pork ribs*
5   cups water
2   teaspoons salt
2   poblano chiles
2   white corn tortillas
1   large white onion, peeled and roughly chopped
4   cloves garlic, peeled
2   serrano chiles (optional for spicier stew),
     stems removed but not seeded
1   bunch cilantro, finely chopped
     (approx. ½ cup, tightly packed)

GARNISHES:
2   ounces Cotija cheese, crumbled
4   radishes, cut into thin rounds
Cilantro sprigs
Lime wedges

In a deep five-quart pot, combine the pork ribs, water, and salt. Bring the water to a boil, then lower the heat to simmer, loosely covered, for an hour and a half or until the meat is tender. While the ribs are simmering, char and peel the poblano chiles as follows: Lightly rub the chiles with oil, char the skins of the chiles over an open flame or under a hot broiler, place the charred chiles in a bowl and cover with a towel, allowing them to steam as they cool. When cool, scrape off the charred skins. Remove and discard the stems and the seeds. Reserve. Lightly toast the corn tortillas over an open flame or in a hot, dry skillet. Tear into small pieces and reserve. When the ribs are tender, remove the ribs to a plate and cover with plastic wrap. Skim off any excess fat. There

should be approximately 3½ cups of broth remaining in the pot. Add the onion, garlic, and optional serrano chiles to the pot. Bring the liquid to a boil and then simmer, uncovered, for ten minutes. Cool the liquid to room temperature. Transfer the cooled mixture to a blender. Add the peeled poblano chiles and tortilla pieces. Blend to form a coarse puree, about 30 seconds.

Transfer the ribs and the puree back to the pot. Bring the liquid to a simmer for an additional 15 to 30 minutes. If the sauce becomes to thick, add additional water. If the sauce is too thin, continue to simmer. Just before serving, stir in the finely chopped cilantro. Serve with crumbled queso fresco, sliced radishes, cilantro sprigs, and lime wedges. Serves 6 to 8.

*Chef's Note: I usually make this dish with bone-in country-style pork ribs, but boneless country-style ribs will work just as well. Cubes of pork shoulder will also work fine. I have also made the dish with pork spare ribs; I cut the whole spare rib into two rib pieces and simmer just like the country-style pork chops. In any case, the meat should be very tender and fall off the bone.

CHICKEN ROASTED WITH GARLIC AND LIMES

SPICY TOMATO RICE WITH RAISINS
AND BANANAS

CHICKEN ROASTED WITH GARLIC
AND LIMES:
1   whole chicken, quartered
1   white onion
8 to 12 cloves garlic, peeled
2   limes
1 to 2 jalapeños (optional)
2   tablespoons extra-virgin olive oil
2   teaspoons salt
½   teaspoon black pepper

Arrange the quartered chicken in a roasting pan large enough to easily hold the chicken. Peel the onion and cut into eighths. Evenly distribute the onion and garlic cloves over the chicken. Cut the limes into quarters. Distribute the lime pieces over the chicken. Slice the jalapeño into thick, round slices and distribute over the chicken. Drizzle the olive oil over the chicken. Sprinkle with the salt and pepper. Broil the chicken within two to three inches of the heating element for approximately 20 minutes or until the chicken is nicely browned. Switch the oven to the bake setting and set the temperature at 300° F. Bake the chicken for 45 minutes. Occasionally spoon some of the juices that collect in the pan over the chicken.

SPICY TOMATO RICE WITH RAISINS
AND BANANAS:
½   white onion, roughly chopped
2   cloves garlic
1   pound tomatoes, Roma or salad
2   tablespoons butter or oil
1   cup rice
¼   cup raisins
1   banana, firm or just slightly under ripe,
     peeled and cut into ½-inch rounds
1½ teaspoon salt
1½ cups canned chicken broth or water
1   jalapeño (optional), seeded and chopped
½   cup chopped cilantro

Prepare the rice by combining the chopped onions, garlic cloves, and whole tomatoes in a small oven-proof pan. Place the ingredients under a hot broiler and broil until the tomatoes are lightly charred, approximately 20 to 30 minutes (note: this can be accomplished while preparing the ingredients for the chicken). Transfer the broiled ingredients to a food processor and process briefly to form a coarse puree. Alternatively, roughly chop the ingredients by hand.

In a sauce pot with a lid, heat the butter or oil over medium-high heat. Add the rice and sauté until lightly toasted (approximately 3 to 5 minutes). Add the raisins and banana and briefly sauté for one minute. Add the chopped roasted tomato mixture, the salt, and the chicken broth. Stir to mix well. Bring the liquid to a near boil then lower the heat to a bare simmer. Cover and cook the rice for approximately 15 minutes. Remove from the heat. Stir in the jalapeño and chopped cilantro.

To serve, transfer the chicken with the onions, garlic, and limes to a serving platter. Pour the juices over the chicken or serve on the side. Serves 6.

kraftsmen

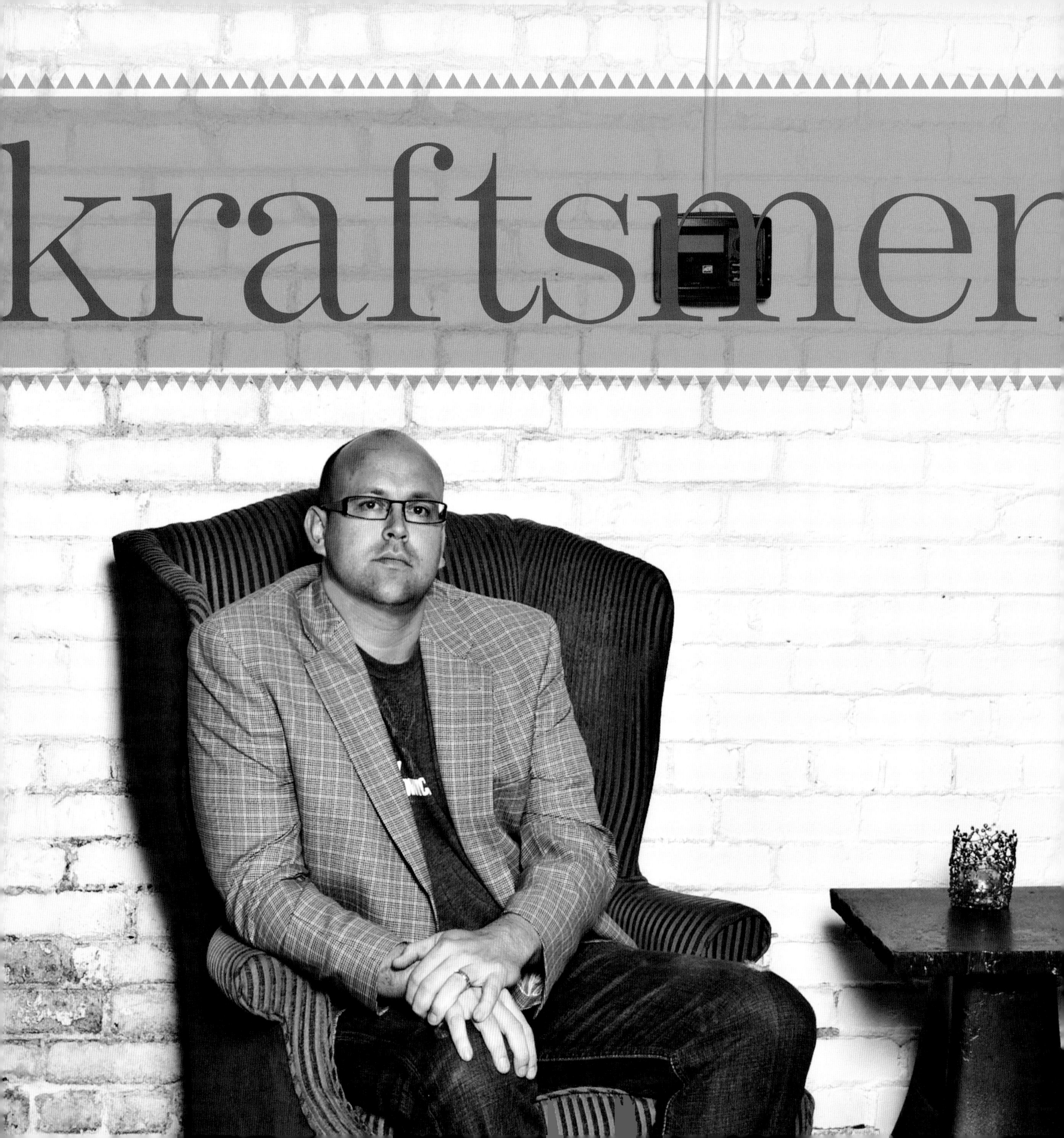

kraftsmen

▼▼▼▼▼▼▼▼▼▼▼▼▼▼▼▼

SCOTT TYCER STARTED HIS CAREER SURROUNDED BY BOOKS AND, in some ways, not a whole lot has changed. In the beginning, Scott filled every available space with the books of a college English major fascinated by literature from what he calls a "theoretical perspective." "I liked Faulkner," he offers, by way of clarification, "but I was never a Faulknerian."

Today, almost two decades later, his office within the landmark building that houses his baking company, Kraftsmen, is most notable for its eight tall stacks of food books along one window. You never know, the stacks remind us, when you might need a chemical dissertation on what makes bread crunchy, chewy, or soft; what helps caviar balance the proper fishiness and saltiness; or exactly how a terrine is different from a tian. As Ring Lardner said what now seems a thousand years ago: You can look it up.

There's a lot you can look up about Scott Tycer, a chef who's earned his share of local, regional, and national media attention since opening his first Houston restaurant in 2001. The Aries days, filled with promise and strife. The Gravitas days, filled with comfort foods and difficult lessons in being a business partner. The Kraftsmen days, when he recaptured Houston's attention mostly with flour and water. A lot. But if that's all you do, you'll never hear Scott remember growing up with a father from very poor conditions and a mother from very rich ones. And you'll never hear him talk about his first adventures with food.

"When I was a child, I sat in the kitchen and asked 'Can I help?'" he remembers. "If it was my grandmother, she'd just say 'No. Sit there and I'll feed you.' If it was my mother, well, my mother was notorious for burning me or cutting me in the process of cooking. There were all these deterrents to cooking: pain, pain, and pain. You might say I chose a profession that was very painful."

With his cerebral approach and his high degree of perfectionism in the kitchen, Scott is one of those Houston-born chefs that everyone assumes has to be from someplace else. If he had the accent, you would quickly tag him as French. And even without one, you are likely to listen to him talk about obscure produce practices or esoteric techniques and rule out any state except California—where he did indeed spend some important years.

But the better you get to know Scott, the more you recognize the telltale signs of a Texan. He loves big foods, big flavors, big ideas—in fact, he insists upon them, even though the servings they produced at Aries, and later at his small eatery called Textile, can be relatively small.

"I'm a firm believer in the historical value of cooking," Scott explains, each closing of one philosophical door flinging open another. "You can make a chicken fried steak in a fine dining restaurant and maybe not even call it chicken fried steak. In your soul, you really love the chicken fried steak you had in that little place 15 or 20 years ago. And you know you can reinvent it in a way that people will really like."

"I'm a firm believer in the historical value of cooking," Scott explains.

Reinvention has always been the core of any Scott Tycer menu, for reasons that become more obvious the more he talks about his life.

Scott's father's side of the family was poor, and he recalls visiting his grandmother in a shotgun-style shack in Corpus Christi. All the same, the foods she cooked for all family gatherings were amazing. Most things, he now admits, relied on heavy saturated fats—lard, chicken fat, bacon fat—but that made even the simplest fried eggs in the morning into something like religious epiphanies. "It was all great," Scott says.

His mother's family in Houston, on the other hand, was well-off, meaning that in the fashion of the day most of the dishes she prepared came direct from the Junior League cookbook. There was a whole string of casseroles, many prepared with canned cream of mushroom soup, what Scott calls "the American velouté of the '50s." One particular casserole, chicken curry with mayonnaise, still turns up on the menu at Textile from time to time. Reinvented. Of course. "That curried chicken casserole," observes the chef who once graced the cover of *Food and Wine* magazine, "is still worthy of the respect I gave it as a child."

One thing he never respected, never considered, never wanted growing up was a job in any kitchen. It never crossed his mind, and in the days before that position delivered celebrity via the media, there was no reason for it to. What pressed him into the restaurant business was the need for cash while studying at UT in Austin. Austin had plenty of restaurants, most of them high-volume, and they were the only places that would hire college students. Without experience, Scott accepted the single job offered to him—as a dishwasher.

After remaining in that steamy, greasy pit longer than he now feels he should have—but proud of the job he did: "I was good and I was fast"—the English major went through a series of moves between the dining room and the kitchen. By the time he'd earned his BA, he'd experienced enough to see that a whole new road was beckoning.

"I had this insubstantial document in my hand," he says. "And on the other hand, I really liked to cook. I got something very immediate and gratifying from that."

Culinary school seemed a good idea, so Scott went off to Portland to pursue a culinary degree. As a side benefit, he met his future wife, Annika, on a backpacking trip through the Cascades in the Pacific Northwest, she fresh out of Stanford business school. And he rose quickly after finishing that program to work in a small, high-end Portland restaurant called Couvron. Jobs came fast and furious throughout this period, barely a year in each place. Within a single two-year period once he moved home to Houston, Scott cooked at the Ritz-Carlton (now the St. Regis), at benjy's, and at Dacapo's, where he worked alongside Charles Clark before that chef went on to create Ibiza and later Catalan.

Reinvention has always been the core of any Scott Tycer menu.

All this diverse hometown experience pointed him to a place even more diverse, San Francisco. His first job there, as dining room chef of the Stanford Park Hotel, pointed him toward the single job that would define and inspire him once he became an entrepreneur. Scott signed on with Wolfgang Puck, arguably the original celeb-chef, when he opened an offshoot of Spago in Palo Alto. In some ways, the job placed him at a crossroads in American food history, since Puck's media-savvy brand was replacing yet another huge name in the same location, the Stars concept created by California cuisine co-founder Jeremiah Tower. Not so shabby for a kid from Houston, cooking on the same burners used by those guys.

Eventually, though, it was time to come home. Scott was a different chef now than he'd been upon heading west, filled with the California gospel of fresh, seasonal, and local, with a side order of organic, sustainable, free-range, and fair trade whenever possible. Ready to conquer Houston in a mere night or two, he was gunning for a shock. The young chef with the sizzling resume got absolutely no interesting job offers when he buzzed back into town. Shock became sadness and sadness became anger. And, you might say, anger became Scott Tycer's first Houston restaurant, Aries.

The place was fine dining, more California-style than Houston-style, and a lot of its biggest fans were food critics from California and New York who propelled Scott into a whirlwind of media fame not always backed up by success as a manager or even in the bank. Before long, many local cooks were afraid to work for him. And even some diners were afraid, since the Great Scott seemed more interested in what he wanted to cook than what they wanted to eat. And he wasn't very shy about telling them so.

"It was tough going those first two years," Scott admits. "I became a little bit of a control freak, especially after my mother was diagnosed with cancer. I couldn't control that, so I tried harder and harder to control every piece of this. I was inflexible. I was petty. And I was young. The existence of that restaurant, start to finish, had a dramatic effect on me."

So did several other important things, all mixed in with his mother's passing. In 2001, the same year he bought the building that became Aries, he and Annika bought their first house and welcomed the first of their two children.

It was Annika, in fact, who finally talked Scott into letting go of Aries, since it was driving him a bit crazy—and crazy never stays at the office. By the time he shut down the restaurant in 2007, he had already opened Gravitas, serving comfort food, and he had launched Kraftsmen Baking to supply local chefs with the finest artisan breads. He had also begun the long recovery toward the "older, gentler Scott" (he jokes about it, but there's no one around who regrets the change) and started dreaming of new projects. Finding an old textile factory in the Houston Heights let him build a permanent home for Kraftsmen.

Day after day, in the hyper-organized workshop he put into the complex, Scott Tycer researches food and wine in all those stacks of books in his office. You might say Scott has gone on to graduate school through his

years as a chef, but he'd be unlikely to tell you in any one word or phrase exactly what his major has been. He might, however, on a good day, let on that he's a little bit happy.

"There is a balance," he offers. "I'm not too self-aware, really. I don't have it all planned out. It might be good to know myself better. But then again, it might just stress me out more."

"It was tough going those first two years. I became a little bit of a control freak, especially after my mother was diagnosed with cancer."

PÂTE BRISÉE:

2 ½ cups all-purpose flour
1   teaspoon salt
1   tablespoon granulated sugar
1   cup (2 sticks) unsalted butter, chilled
    and cut into 1-inch pieces
¼ to ½ cup ice water

The trick to a nice brisée is to work it as little as possible, to avoid building any gluten and to get a beautiful flake.

Throw the dry ingredients into a food processor and pulse until mixed. Add all the cold butter and pulse until a course meal forms, pulsing quickly to avoid the butter becoming warm. Turn processor on low and add water until the dough just comes together. Wrap and refrigerate for an hour.

Preheat the oven to 350° F. Roll dough as thin as you like and line a mold, such as a cupcake pan. Line the shells with parchment paper and cover with uncooked beans or pie weights to bake. Bake until golden brown, about 10 to 12 minutes. Let cool to room temperature before use.

BALSAMIC VINAIGRETTE:

½   cup balsamic vinegar
1   egg yolk
2   teaspoons Dijon mustard
½   shallot
½   clove garlic
Salt and pepper to taste
1 ½ cups grapeseed oil

Blend everything except the oil in a blender or food processor. Slowly add the oil until all is mixed well. (Watch the temperature of the liquid here. This recipe is pretty bulletproof, but if the mix gets too hot, it will separate.)

BACON VELOUTÉ:

5   strips high-quality bacon, such as Neuske's
½   shallot, chopped
1   clove garlic, cut in half
2   cups milk
1   tablespoon all-purpose flour
1   tablespoon cool butter

Chop the bacon and stir in a pan over medium heat until the fat is rendered. Then add the shallot, garlic, and milk. Cook just until bubbly. Blend the mixture until smooth, then return to the pan. Thicken with a beurre manier, by using your fingers to knead the flour with the butter and then adding it.

8   additional strips bacon, cut in cubes
1   shallot, minced
1   bunch collard greens, chopped
1   tablespoon balsamic vinegar
2   heads frisée, chopped
Quail (or chicken) eggs, poached

In a hot sauté pan, render the bacon until brown. Stir in the shallot and cook for 1 minute. Add the collard greens with the balsamic vinegar and stir for about 5 minutes. Add the frisée and remove the pan from the heat. Drain on a paper towel.

To make the tart, fill the baked tart shells about halfway up the sides with the Bacon Velouté, then the rest of the way with the bacon-greens mixture. Top with the poached eggs and serve immediately. Makes 12 to 15 tarts.

SUMMER SQUASH SALAD WITH GOAT CHEESE

2 tablespoons goat cheese
2 teaspoons minced shallots, divided
1 teaspoon minced fresh parsley
1 yellow squash, very thinly sliced
1 zucchini, very thinly sliced
½ shallot, very thinly sliced
1 cup champagne vinegar
1 quart apple juice, reduced to ½ cup over high heat
1 tablespoon chopped fresh tarragon
Juice of 1 lemon
2 teaspoons Dijon mustard
1 cup grapeseed oil
Salt and pepper to taste
1 apple, diced
Dehydrated fennel chips for garnish (optional)
Reduced balsamic vinaigrette (optional)

Using your fingers, combine the goat cheese with 1 teaspoon of the minced shallots and parsley. Use plastic wrap to roll into a smooth cigar. Refrigerate until ready to use.

Combine the squash, zucchini, and the sliced shallot in a bowl with the champagne vinegar, and let marinate for 1 to 2 hours. Make the apple vinaigrette by blending the reduced apple juice with the remaining 1 teaspoon shallot, tarragon, lemon juice, and Dijon mustard. With the blender running on low, slowly drizzle in the grapeseed oil until incorporated. Season to taste with salt and pepper.

To serve, arrange the marinated vegetables on a plate and garnish with diced apple. Slice the goat cheese into small wheels and add to the presentation. Spoon a small amount of the apple vinaigrette around the plate. Garnish with dehydrated fennel chips and reduced balsamic vinegar, if desired. Serves 4.

GARLIC CREAM:
1   head garlic
1   shallot
2   cups heavy cream
4   sprigs thyme
1   cup water

Cut garlic and shallot in half, and place all ingredients in a sauce pot. Simmer until reduced by about one third. Strain and set sauce aside.

MIATAKE MUSHROOM SAUTÉ:
4   tablespoons (½ stick) butter, unsalted
8   ounces miatake mushrooms
     (or regular oyster mushrooms), cut into strips
½   shallot, minced
1   clove garlic, minced
½   cup sherry
¼   cup chicken stock

Over medium heat, melt butter and let brown slightly. Add the mushrooms and sauté until they start to brown. Add shallot and garlic, cooking until translucent. Add thyme, sherry, and stock. Reduce until the pan is almost dry (you have to watch this here; keep stirring or you'll burn something). Let mushrooms cool.

PAN-SEARED SALMON:
4   salmon fillets, 5 ounces each
1   cup rice flour
3   tablespoons grapeseed oil
1   tablespoon unsalted butter

Red wine demi-glace (optional)
   (available at gourmet food stores)
Warmed snails (optional)

To complete the dish, combine garlic cream and mushrooms in a sauce pan and bring to a simmer.

Preheat a sauté pan over medium-high heat until very hot. Coat the salmon with rice flour. Add the grapeseed oil to the hot pan, then add salmon, skin side down. (Be sure to score the salmon skins so the skin stays crisp). Once sides of fish start to slightly brown, add the butter. When the edges get golden brown, flip the salmon. Baste with the butter, cooking for about 2 minutes.

Ladle the mushrooms and cream into shallow bowls, then top with the seared salmon. If you like add a swizzle of the red wine demi-glace for presentation. We often also garnish this dish with warmed snails, but it's hardly necessary. Serves 4.

VEAL TENDERLOIN WITH BEEF LIVER CRUMBLIES AND SERRANO FOAM

BEEF LIVER CRUMBLIES:
¼ pound beef liver
1 cup milk
¼ cup all-purpose flour
Salt to taste
About ¾ tablespoon butter for frying

Soak beef liver in milk overnight. Freeze the liver. Once frozen solid, grate using the big eye on your grater. Toss with flour, and a touch of salt. Pan-fry in the butter. Drain on paper towels.

SERRANO FOAM:
½ pound serrano peppers, diced
2 shallots
2 tablespoons smoked paprika
1 clove garlic
3 cups water
2 tablespoons soy lecithin
   (available at nutrition stores)

Simmer all ingredients except the lecithin in a sauce pan for about an hour, until the serrano gets soft. Blend together. You will probably have to add some more water to get it to puree. Strain the pulp through a chinois, pressing with a spoon to drain all the liquid. Add the lecithin and buzz with a stick blender. Tilt the vessel at an angle to maximize the incorporation of air, making a foam.

MOLE:
3 poblano peppers, seeded and chopped
6 ancho peppers, seeded to your preferred spice level
1 red onion, roughly chopped
4 cloves garlic
2 ounces Valrhona chocolate (70% cacao)
1 tablespoon brown sugar
3 cups water
½ cup pumpkin seeds, toasted
1 splash sherry vinegar

Combine all ingredients in a sauce pan and simmer until all vegetables have cooked through. Blend together, with a splash of sherry vinegar, until smooth.

VEAL TENDERLOIN:
1 (2 to 3 pound) veal tenderloin, cut in 2½-inch pieces
2 tablespoons unsalted butter

To build the dish, pan-fry the veal in a big knob of butter until medium rare. Drain. Heat the mole. It has a nice body for fancy plating, so you can do a line on the plate, or a swirly or spoon smear.

Place veal on the plate, top with the foam, and sprinkle the crumblies.

Chef's Note: This is a pretty expensive plate, but might be an easy one to start learning some of the plating aesthetics we like to play with. Serves 4.

¾   *cup granulated sugar*
¾   *cup plus ½ cup light brown sugar*
1   *stick unsalted butter*
6   *cups heavy cream*
15   *eggs*
¾   *loaf crusty bread, preferably Kraftsmen, cut into small cubes*
Vanilla ice cream
Crushed toffee bar

Preheat the oven to 350° F.

Heat granulated sugar and ¾ cup light brown sugar, butter, and one cup of the cream in large pot. Heat until sugar melts and begins to caramelize. Slowly add remaining cream, whisking after each addition. Let boil for 5 minutes. In a mixing bowl, whisk the eggs. Gradually add in the hot cream mixture.

Spray a large baking pan with nonstick spray and line with parchment paper. Place bread into the pan and press down. Pour pudding mix into the pan with bread. Press down on bread so that it absorbs the mixture. Top with remaining brown sugar. Cover with foil and bake for 45 minutes. Remove foil and continue baking for 30 more minutes. Remove from oven and cut into 3 x 3¼-inch squares. Plate individually and serve warm with ice cream and crushed toffee. Serves about 10.

t'afia

SOME ADMIRERS SEEM BETTER ABLE TO PICTURE MONICA POPE in the garden than in the kitchen. But then again, the entire saga of how a Texas girl born to an American military family in Germany grew up to be "The Alice Waters of Houston"—with a weekly farmers' market in her own *restaurant*, no less—seems to surprise no one quite as much as it does Monica Pope.

"For all these years, I was the weird one," she reflects, thinking specifically of her efforts to make the food she ate and served more seasonal, more organic, and more local—"passionately local," the menu proclaims. "Now sometimes everybody around me, all the cheffies in these major restaurants, are doing the same things I've been doing for years," she laughs, "which I think means I'm normal."

There is an intriguing creative tension inside Monica, and the struggle between "weird" and "normal" isn't the half of it. There's also the struggle between the firebrand, the visionary, the revolutionary with a Big Message—and the self-deprecating restaurant cook who wants to keep her eyes on the stove and just be left alone. Even at her most expansive, Monica doesn't seem entirely comfortable "being" Alice Waters, the woman who turned America's eyes to a different way of cooking and eating at her Chez Panisse in Berkeley. First and foremost, Monica's every glance seems to remind us, that was *Berkeley*. And this is Houston.

She sits with her signature short, spiked hair and a clean white T-shirt at a table in her pleasantly minimalist restaurant called t'afia (named after a Provençal fortified wine), her curly-haired six-year-old daughter, Lili, coloring a picture with markers at the nearest table to her right. Before the end of today's conversation, Lili will ask to do something she apparently does often: produce her own blend by having spice after spice brought out from the kitchen then smashing them together with a heavy mortar and pestle. Almost instantly, the empty dining room smells like a bazaar in Marrakech.

It's an understandable mistake when Monica speaks of "college in Baltimore, Europe, and California," for that is the way she lived it. Her school, called John Goucher, was quite stationary in Baltimore, chosen for its excellent program in medical illustration. However, Monica picked up a degree in creative writing there anyway, winning honors status for her thesis. Still, the "end of education" was anything but, propelling her into two-plus years of cooking in England and Greece, followed by several even more formative years in San Francisco. It was all one course of study, according to Monica.

"I think I wanted to run away from reality in some ways," she says now, particularly of the European period. "But I just got through all the icky, hard kitchen-reality stuff over there. I was just letting that dream find its way. After all, I worked for two days for my dad in his law office—and that was about two days too many."

As her life became more and more culinary—and therefore, less and less literary—Monica found herself thinking about her grandmother. She had spent considerable time, deliberately perhaps, cooking beside the older

"For all these years, I was the weird one," she reflects, thinking specifically of her efforts to make the food she ate and served more seasonal, more organic, and more local—"passionately local," the menu proclaims.

woman in Hutchinson, Kansas. Now, as she looked back, all that food preparation came to represent a good deal more. "I was interested in what she had done for the family," Monica remembers.

The chef-to-be, fresh from her overseas adventures, spent nearly two years in San Francisco. In culinary terms, for her, those proved a virtual lifetime. In northern California, she was exposed to the then-latest about food, how it was done, and what it might mean. Ironically considering her later honorific, Monica never worked for Alice Waters, though Chez Panisse certainly shared her favorite dining list with places like Zuni and Campanille. On the road to what she now sarcastically shortens to "French-Ital-Cal" cooking, she spent time learning from Margaret Fox up in Mendocino and Cindy Pawlcyn back in San Francisco, who Monica reports "wanted to have like 20 restaurants by the time she was 40." Truth be told, Monica figured she'd settle for one.

By the time her parents told her the oil-driven recession that had crippled Houston throughout the '80s was over, she was ready to come home and try her luck. Yet she was still a long way from thinking the city in which she'd grown up was ready for anything she'd been preparing in San Francisco. "I didn't think I could," Monica says, "and I didn't think this region would allow you to do that style of food. Twenty years ago, the best I could do was: Let's make this stuff taste real."

And "real" she would make it taste, initially at the Quilted Toque, named after the cap her grandmother wore when she was cooking. It was during this period of operating her own first restaurant that the then-ridiculous notion that Monica was the new Alice Waters came to be. Diners, she interprets, saw a woman chef who just moved here from California—even though "here" was home—with a goal of changing the way people eat. Alice Waters, people announced. "It was just kinda funny," Monica announces now.

Her first time out of the chute, Monica kept the Quilted Toque for two years, from 1992 to 1994, serving what she now acknowledges was her read on "patchwork-melting pot" cuisine. And her read would only deep and intensify through the ten years that followed, as she pressed her next place, Boulevard Bistrot in the heart of Houston's bohemian Montrose section, to the forefront of American fine-dining restaurants.

> By the time her parents told her the oil-driven recession that had crippled Houston throughout the '80s was over, she was ready to come home and try her luck.

Along the way, her once "weird" beliefs about cooking and especially fresh ingredients came to find echoes all over town. One day, for instance, Robert Del Grande of Café Annie and Tim Keating, then of the Four Seasons, invited Monica to join the Chefs Collaborative, a California-sounding notion to benefit Urban Harvest. That pushed her to the point of having a swirl of local farmers in her restaurant one day. It was the turning point, she says. After that day, after talking to growers committed to local and organic foods, her motto for life was formed: Eat Where Your Food Lives.

"People still talk about that day, and I still buy from several of the farmers who were there," Monica says. "But not every chef was going to embrace it. A couple of them told me I was nuts, by the way; but I just kept on in a small way back at Boulevard. I'd buy these little bags of stuff that somebody would bring me to try. I'd put whatever it was on the blackboard and just make 10 specials or 15 specials. We were all about that local stuff. But at the end of every day, the blackboard just got erased. So when we moved over here, we put it on the menu."

The place Monica calls "over here" is t'afia, set amid the transformative growth of Houston's vibrant Midtown. She and her partner, Andrea Lazar, opened t'afia in 2004, just about the time Houston was hosting the Super Bowl. Rather quickly, Monica's work to call attention to a local farmers' market—she was there every Saturday—pointed her closer to home. To the delight of area growers and other food professionals, the Midtown Farmers Market came to call t'afia its permanent home.

And the evolution, which for Monica is synonymous with self-discovery, continues into the future, indefinitely. For the first two or three years, t'afia offered all its most exciting local farm-to-table creations on a special tasting menu each night. But then Monica began to ponder whether this was the right idea but the wrong message. Such foods were meant to appear throughout our diets, she decided, not merely when we spring for a famous chef's tasting menu. Today the menu at t'afia features local, organic produce all over the map, in the least expected of places, and often as though we are taking such things almost for granted. Hope really *does* spring eternal.

By the day of our conversation, the old local market tasting menu had been expanded to include your choice of five courses for $45, each pairable with a Texas wine for $20 more. There is a list of "bites" (nifty little things like

To the delight of area growers and other food professionals, the Midtown Farmers Market came to call t'afia its permanent home.

Medjool dates stuffed with chorizo and wrapped in bacon, and chickpea "fries" with red and green sauces). Next up in size are the "small plates," a bit like Spanish tapas—cream of mushroom soup with balsamic vinegar; mushroom pate with vanilla bean vinaigrette and crostini; or spaghetti with edamame, corn, tomato, and chicken meats.

Even though the "many tastes" approach works best at t'afia, there are a few official "entrees." Some are upper-crust, like the chermoula scallops with bulghur and lemon sauce, but there's a wildly popular burger as well, its patty a mix of ribeye and sirloin—then totally cheffed-up with lavender-black pepper pizzette where the bun should be, plus lemon aioli and shoestring potatoes. Or you can go back to square one, at the bottom of the menu in this case, and mix-and-match a protein with a side with a sauce.

The evolution Monica has enjoyed at t'afia in recent years has been personal as well as professional. Long tending to be shy (despite the usual celeb-chef public performances), Monica now finds herself each Saturday teaching a cooking class upstairs from her farmers' market. Just a few simple dishes, she insists, straightforward ways a home cook might enjoy the good and good-for-you products on sale below. Not only has she learned to be comfortable in front of a live audience, but she's learned to live with the lesson Julia Child taught us all on TV nearly a half-century ago.

"They get to see me screw up," Monica says. "I mean, not in a major way, but just something that doesn't work the way it was supposed to." She looks over at Lili, who continues to assault the air with aromatic fireworks, as though hoping the message will someday get through. "And they understand that it's OK if you screw up."

In the hard-edged, hard-won vocabulary of Monica Pope, the so-called Alice Waters of Houston, that's saying a mouthful.

Long tending to be shy, Monica now finds herself each Saturday teaching a cooking class upstairs from her farmers' market.

ENDIVE, CREMINI, SPICED PECANS, AND BLEU CHEESE SALAD

WITH WHITE TRUFFLE–WHITE BALSAMIC VINAIGRETTE

WHITE TRUFFLE–WHITE BALSAMIC VINAIGRETTE:

1	tablespoon whole-grain mustard		¼	cup white balsamic vinegar
2	tablespoons minced shallot		¾	cup grapeseed oil
2	teaspoons chopped fresh thyme		¼	cup white truffle oil
2	teaspoons kosher salt			Salt and pepper

Blend all ingredients in a food processor or blender until smooth.

SPICED PECANS:

2 ½ cups water			¼	teaspoon ground red pepper
¼	cup Wholesome Sweeteners sugar, split into two ⅛-cup portions		1	cup Rio Grande organic pecans
				Oil for frying

Combine the water, ⅛ cup of the sugar, and cayenne in a pot and bring to a boil. Add the pecans and continue boiling for 5 minutes. Strain the nuts. In a stainless steel bowl, toss the still-wet nuts with the rest of the sugar. Heat the oil in a pan until it reaches 350 degrees. Fry the nuts in two batches for 2 to 3 minutes. Lay on a sheet pan to cool.

SALAD:

2 whole endives (Belgian, white, or red), cut in half, with core removed and sliced on bias about ½-inch thick

8 whole Texas cremini mushrooms, stems removed and quartered

4 tablespoons Veldhuizen's Bosque bleu cheese, crumbled (or Paula Lambert's Deep Ellum Bleu or Pure Luck's Hopelessly Bleu)

½ cup spiced Rio Grande organic pecans, chopped

Kosher salt and white pepper

Slice ingredients right before serving, mix, and dress liberally with the dressing. Once plated, sprinkle salad with salt and pepper. Serves 4.

WILD GULF SHRIMP DUMPLINGS WITH KAFFIR LIME-GREEN CURRY SAUCE

WILD GULF SHRIMP DUMPLINGS:

1 ¼ pound wild American shrimp, peeled and deveined (tail and head off)

Salt and cayenne pepper to taste

2 teaspoons paprika

3 tablespoons kaffir lime leaves, chopped

1 package wonton wrappers, small size, about 3-inches square, usually in produce or freezer section

1 beaten egg, hormone-antibiotic-free

Finely chop shrimp by hand; don't "puree" them. Add salt, cayenne, paprika, and kaffir lime leaves, saving some kaffir lime leaves for garnish. Mix together well. With wet hands form one 1-inch ball with the mixture and blanch in boiling water for 3 minutes. Taste to make sure seasoning is right; adjust if necessary. Wet hands again and continue to form 1-inch balls until completed. Blanch, in batches of 10 or 15, in boiling water for 3 minutes.

To make the dumplings you will need one wonton wrapper for each dumpling. Put the boiled shrimp balls into the middle of each wrapper, brush some beaten egg around the edges, and then gather the edges together (just above the shrimp ball), as if making a small package. Set aside.

KAFFIR LIME–GREEN CURRY SAUCE:

1 tablespoon coriander seeds

1 cup chopped cilantro

1 chopped shallot

1 clove garlic, chopped

2 jalapeños, seeded and chopped

2 kaffir lime leaves

¼ teaspoon ground pepper

1 teaspoon ground nutmeg

1 cup grapeseed or pomace olive oil (NOT extra-virgin olive oil)

⅔ tablespoon grated fresh ginger

1 tablespoon fresh-squeezed lemon juice

Salt

Toast coriander seeds, let cool, and grind in a spice grinder. Combine with all other ingredients and process in a food processor until desired consistency is reached.

To assemble, place dumplings in boiling, salted water for 1 minute. Remove the dumplings with a slotted spoon and place 5 to 6 in the middle of a bowl. Spoon some kaffir lime-green curry sauce over the dumplings. Garnish with julienned kaffir lime leaves. Makes 25 to 30 dumplings.

BALSAMIC CARAMEL BEEF WITH SHIITAKE MUSHROOMS,

ORGANIC RICE, TOASTED COCONUT, AND GOMASHIO

GOMASHIO:

2   tablespoons plus 2 teaspoons black sesame seeds
2   tablespoons plus 2 teaspoons white sesame seeds
1   sheet nori
2   teaspoons kosher salt
1   teaspoon crushed red pepper
2   cups Lowell Farms organic jasmine rice

CARAMEL SAUCE:

2   cups organic chicken or vegetable stock
2   tablespoons kecap manis*
2   tablespoons balsamic vinegar
1   tablespoon Wholesome Sweeteners organic sugar
6   cloves organic garlic, peeled and thinly sliced

BEEF AND SHIITAKE MUSHROOMS:

2   cups stemmed Texas shiitake mushrooms
2   tablespoons grapeseed oil
2   tablespoons kosher salt
1   tablespoon freshly ground pepper
1 ½ to 2 pounds Texas beef, cut into 1 ½-inch cubes,
     seasoned with salt and pepper (all-natural,
     no hormones, no antibiotics)
3   tablespoons organic butter
¼   cup unsweetened shaved coconut, toasted, to garnish

Make the gomashio first. Toast sesame seeds in a sauté pan. Let cool. Grind in a spice grinder until fine but not powder-like. Toast nori, let cool, and pulse in a spice grinder. Nori should not be a powder, but small flakes. Add to ground seed mixture with salt and red pepper flakes. Set aside.

Cook the rice as per the instructions on the package.

Keep warm until ready to serve. While waiting for your rice to cook, combine all ingredients for the caramel sauce and set aside.

Sauté the mushrooms in grapeseed oil, season with salt and pepper, and set aside. Sear the seasoned beef cubes in a sauté pan that you have drizzled with grapeseed oil for 2 to 3 minutes on each side. This will cook the beef only halfway. Do not put too much beef in the pan at one time; make sure there's just one layer in the pan. Do as many batches of beef as you need, wiping the pan clean after two batches.

Put all of the seared beef, along with the mushrooms, back in the pan. Pour in ½ cup caramel sauce and bring to a boil. Cook over medium-high heat, shaking pan occasionally; after about 2 minutes, add the butter. Continue to shake pan occasionally, until the sauce has slightly thickened, about 2 minutes more (add more caramel sauce in ½ cup increments if sauce starts to thicken too much).

To assemble, mound rice in the middle of a plate. Top with beef, mushrooms, and balsamic-caramel sauce. Garnish with toasted coconut and gomashio. Variations: This recipe is also great with beets and toasted walnuts instead of the mushrooms. It also works with other proteins, such as chicken and shrimp. Serves 4.

*Chef's Note: If you cannot find kecap manis, you can make your own sweet soy sauce by combining one tablespoon soy sauce, one tablespoon molasses, and one tablespoon sugar.

CRUST:

2   cups nuts, usually walnuts, ground in food processor
½   cup unsalted butter, melted
½   cup sugar
½   cup flour

CHEESECAKE:

3   pounds cream cheese
3   cups sugar
5   tablespoons cornstarch
6   whole eggs
3   vanilla beans, scraped

Preheat the oven to 350° F.

Mix the ingredients for the crust and press into an 8-inch springform pan. Wrap pan base in foil. Bake for about 10 minutes. It will be lightly colored and puff slightly.

In a stand mixer with a paddle attachment, cream the cream cheese (you can substitute up to ⅓ with a different cheese, such as goat or fromage blanc) with sugar and cornstarch, making sure all the cream cheese is incorporated by periodically scraping the bottom of the bowl with a spatula. Add the eggs one at a time, mixing after each addition, followed by the vanilla bean. The mixture should be very fluffy.

Bake in a bain marie in the 350-degree oven until lightly brown, about 20 to 30 minutes. (Note: a knife will not come out clean; the mixture on the knife will be gooey, not liquid-y.)

Variations: lemon-blackberry with pinenut crust; white chocolate with hazelnut crust; mandarin orange with pistachio crust; fig puree with walnut crust

reef | stella sola

reef | stella sola

▼▼▼▼▼▼▼▼▼▼▼▼▼▼▼▼▼▼▼▼▼▼▼

HOUSTON-BORN BRYAN CASWELL, fresh from more than two years at the Culinary Institute of America, sneaked into the Trump Tower in Manhattan via the loading dock, flashed a vaguely official-looking card to anybody who seemed interested, and finally spotted the legendary chef behind the Michelin three-starred restaurant inside—Jean-Georges Vongerichten.

"I introduced myself," Bryan remembers, "and he just kept on walking. That was Jean-Georges. I was nervous. I was shaking. I probably only did it because I was half-drunk from the night before." He thinks back, with more than a little disbelief. "Here I was, this big, slow-talking redneck from Texas. It still amazes me I was one of the guys he eventually chose to push forward."

Whatever Bryan's sobriety level at the time, that first non-meeting between one world-famous European chef and an American chef just starting out proved to be the birth of a working relationship that would last years and span several continents. It would take Bryan through all of Jean-George's eateries in New York City, the Bahamas, Las Vegas, and as far away as Hong Kong and Bangkok. Finally, in one of life's stranger twists, it would bring him home to Houston, where an even larger culinary destiny awaited him.

With both parents from French-influenced south Louisiana—a mother from Opelousas, a father from Morgan City—Bryan's early life in Houston seemed forever perched on the banks of the Sabine River. He grew up understanding intuitively that the state line was more important to governments than to people, to real culture. And his devotion to the basic life-loving tenets of the Cajuns felt as much at home in Houston—sometimes called The Bayou City, after all—as it would have been on any bayou between Lake Charles and New Orleans.

"Those are people," Bryan says from vast personal experience, "who cook, eat, and hang out with family and extended family. Growing up, I spent weeks at hunting and fishing camps, with whole days focused on killing what we were going to eat that night. When I was two years old and it was my birthday, I could invite two people over and my family would invite about sixty. And believe me, they were still going long after I had to go to bed."

The Texas chef is now nationally famous for his lush foam-green seafood restaurant called Reef, not to mention his funky slider-and-fry joint dubbed Little Bigs or his Texas-Tuscan concept called Stella Sola (Lone Star, get it?). Bryan stumbled badly in college—stumbled backwards into his true calling, that is. According to Bryan, it took him five years at Texas Tech and Blinn College to amass one and a half hours of credit, spread out over thousands of hours laboring in restaurants as a busboy, dishwasher, waiter, and cook. The tip potential kept his eyes on positions in the front of the house, but by the time he'd worked in two Houston Italian favorites— Damian's and D'Amico's—he had started to fall in love with cooking.

Bryan's father picked up on his fledgling career interest almost before he did, right alongside the need for some kind of serious culinary education. His research into many programs led to the conclusion that his son

"Growing up, I spent weeks at hunting and fishing camps, with whole days focused on killing what we were going to eat that night."

should consider only two cooking schools in the world: the Swiss Hotel School in Lausanne or the Culinary Institute of America in Hyde Park, New York. Europe had its allure, of course, and indeed its rich layering of cuisines would come to inspire Bryan soon enough. But an education at the CIA seemed easier to pull off, especially with its promise of "externships" all over the world, starting in the nearby world of Manhattan.

It was that island, in fact, that provided Bryan with his first serious inkling of what a gifted chef's life can be. His official externship was joined through this period by largely unofficial efforts to learn from some of the best chefs in New York. "I'd come in from Hyde Park on the weekends," he remembers. "I did *stages* at maybe 15 different restaurants. Sometimes I'd just show up with my whites and my knives and work the night. It's better to be a potato peeler in a great restaurant than the sous chef of a mediocre one." This attitude propelled him to Spain for his official CIA externship, spending six months in the fabled kitchen of Chef Jose Muneisa at Via Veneto in Barcelona.

Union Pacific in Manhattan was Bryan's first real job out of culinary school, and he worked every station during the year he spent there under celeb-chef Rocco DiSpirito. And with that restaurant displayed on his resume, alongside Charlie Palmer's Aureole, Alfred Portale's Gotham Bar & Grill, and Wayne Nish's March, even the great Jean-Georges was prepared to take the young man a bit seriously. Seven years and several countries followed, highlighted not only by Jean-Georges's wild array of eateries in New York—Jean-Georges at the Trump Tower, Vong, and several others—but by opening Dune at the posh Ocean Club in the Bahamas, then helping open other Jean-Georges restaurants in Hong Kong and Bangkok.

"He taught me balance, on the plate and in my life," Bryan says now. "His energy level is unparalleled. He likes all kinds of things: design, lighting, clothes, points of service, how to handle employees. Without balance, your life won't make sense."

This balance sustained Bryan through all his travels for Jean-Georges, though once he became a husband and a father, he found his balance elsewhere too. Sooner or later, he knew, he wanted to come home. And home in the Jean-Georges organization meant New York City. With the business disruption caused by the terrorist attacks of 9/11, however, finding a good spot cooking in the Big Apple seemed unlikely for some time to come. For Bryan, as for many people whose lives or careers were traumatized by 9/11, it suddenly seemed time to go home.

Back in Houston, Bryan signed on as a research and development chef for the Pappas family, a huge and hugely successful constellation of restaurant concepts ranging from one high-end steakhouse to casual

> "It's better to be a potato peeler in a great restaurant than the sous chef of a mediocre one."

seafood, burgers, Tex-Mex, and Cajun. He says he learned more from the Pappas management program than he ever knew he didn't know, but he also recognized that time was running out for some kind of bold and decisive move that would define Bryan Caswell as a chef. The clock, as it happened, took a big jump forward when Jean-Georges called him again.

The New York–based chef was eyeing a high-profile project in Houston, of all places, a signature restaurant within a former bank, part of a hotel to be called Icon. Jean-Georges was planning to open Bank, and he thought Bryan was just the top chef for the job.

Though Bank faded from the scene after several years, especially after Bryan had departed, it's important to remember its excitement at the start. For one thing, it was unusual for Houston to get a "celeb-chef" restaurant at all, such places typically going to tourist-heavy dining scenes like Las Vegas or Orlando. The Houston dining scene has always relied almost completely on locals, making the satisfaction of repeat customers essential for a place's survival. Plus, the food served at Bank, for many locals, represented the plated invitation to join a larger world of foie gras and caviar, things they'd tasted during *their* travels to New York or San Francisco, not to mention hand-picked produce, seafoods, and meats.

Bank provided Bryan with three years of constant effort and constant learning, from Jean-Georges himself of course but most of all from his Houston customers. Night after night, his menu experiments produced the ultimate profile of his hometown's homegrown taste—what they loved, what they hated, what they'd never lift

to their mouths. To Bryan, now slowly forming his own vision outside the mantle of Jean-Georges, this profile was the one thing he'd always been looking for. "If you can't get people to eat the food, to like the food and come back again and order it, then what you're doing doesn't make any sense," says Bryan. "It helped me understand what was right for Houston."

At Bank, the executive chef worked closely with Hotel Icon food and beverage director Bill Floyd, especially when it came to Bill's true passion, fine wine. Before long, the two professionals were discussing their dream of a new seafood restaurant, one that would be high-end without ever being snooty, one that would serve the most interesting wines from all over the world without ever failing to give excellent value, and one that would blossom under their constant presence and care, unlike the new breed of upscale chain concepts that were creeping in from the upscale Houston suburbs.

The one-word restaurant Bank evolved into another one-word restaurant once Bryan and Bill left the Icon. The seafood place called Reef was born.

The two were lucky they knew what they were doing, since the crowds at Reef's doors from Day One didn't give them time to figure anything out. Seemingly overnight, the eatery's 175 seats were full, right along with the 40 seats in the bar, the 35 outside, and the 50 treated as private dining. Most guests seemed to prefer a table with one view of the open kitchen—where Bryan could always be spotted working beneath his old-style orange Houston Astros baseball cap (no toques allowed, apparently)—and another view of Bill's towering "wall of wine." As Reef's seafood-wonderland menu came together, Bryan and Bill worked together on selecting the wines the only way they knew how.

"If you can't get people to eat the food, to like the food and come back again and order it, then what you're doing doesn't make any sense," says Bryan.

"We tasted every wine together before we opened," Bryan recalls with an aw-shucks grin. "Bill and I are completely different kinds of wine drinkers. I like whites, and he practically wouldn't even taste them. We wanted to make our wines affordable, selling a bottle for $35 when it's $60 every place else. This wine, we said, is going to be our marketing. I believe in ready, drinkable wines right now."

The wines they chose are meant to pair magnificently with creations from the menu 's opening section called Rare, a kind of Gulf Coast sushi bar that broadens into Italian *crudos* and lime-splashed Mexican *tiraditos*, as well as with cooked appetizers ranging from mussels steamed in Shiner Bock and toasted ancho pepper to Bryan's rich, dark-rouxed seafood gumbo with hyper-aromatic Texmati rice. There's no shortage of meat on Reef's menu, but most guests inspired by the evening light flicking through the sea-green setting surrender to the power of suggestion. Entree favorites include the seafood "hot pot" with fingerling potatoes, the Thai-crazed whole fish, and the redfish "on the half shell," served with fried mac-and-cheese. No matter what people order, a lot of them add the fried mac-and-cheese.

Not surprisingly, with Bryan's upbringing along the Gulf of Mexico, Reef's menu is a Texas fisherman's fantasy. In fact, talking with Bryan about individual dishes, you get the feeling he wishes he had time to go out on the blue-gray Gulf waters and reel in each fish individually. While knowing all too well his customers' preferences, which he runs through like a mantra as "snapper, grouper, shrimp," Bryan has emerged as a leader in the movement to spotlight delicious Gulf fish that commercial fishermen long tossed aside because nobody knew to buy them. This isn't merely good cooking, Bryan says, but the only way to preserve nature's bounty for future generations of chefs, diners, and fishermen. People, in other words, like Bryan Caswell.

"If you spread it out a little bit, it gives the other species a chance," he says, and anyone listening can picture this chef, finally a celebrity in his own right, not only cooking on the line at Reef but fishing beneath the same well-loved Astros cap. "Variety is the spice of life, and the same thing every night is never good. Listen, I want to fish in the Gulf of Mexico till the day I die. And I want my kids to do the same."

GRAPEFRUIT:

2   red grapefruits, peel and pith removed,
     peel reserved and fruit sectioned
1   Thai chile, minced
Extra-virgin olive oil
Salt

To prepare the grapefruit dust, preheat the oven to 200° F. Bring the peelings to a boil in cold water and remove from the heat. Repeat this process two more times. When the water boils for the third time, add one part sugar to three parts water and blanch peelings again. Strain, arrange the peels on a sheet pan with a silpat, and dry the peels until they are brittle. Cool and grind to make powder.

For the grapefruit sections, gently mix all of the ingredients without breaking up the grapefruit sections. Marinate at least one hour before using.

AGRA DOLCE:

½   cup rice vinegar
½   cup palm sugar
½   cup grapefruit juice

For the agra dolce, warm the rice vinegar, add the palm sugar, and stir until the sugar melts. Add the grapefruit juice. Remove from the heat, cool, and reserve in squirt bottle.

GARLIC BRUSCHETTA:

¼   pound unsalted butter, softened
½   cup chopped parsley
6   cloves garlic
Salt and pepper
Sourdough bread

Make the garlic bruschetta by blending all the ingredients except the bread in a food processor. Roll the flavored butter into a log using plastic wrap, and chill in the refrigerator. Slice the bread, and smear each slice with the chilled flavored butter. Toast just before serving the fish.

RED SNAPPER:

1   pound fresh red snapper, sliced paper-thin
Sea salt
Cilantro to taste, cut in a fine chiffonade
Mint leaves to taste, cut in a fine chiffonade
White pepper

To serve, arrange snapper slices on a plate, patting down to create a single thin layer. Cover with 2 tablespoons grapefruit marinade and top with 1 tablespoon of the agra dolce and sea salt. Dust plate with grapefruit dust. Garnish with the garlic bruschetta. Scatter the cilantro and mint chiffonades and the white pepper on top to season the fish. Serves 6 to 8.

CORN PUDDING:

6   *large ears of corn, shucked*
1   *tablespoon vegetable oil*
2   *tablespoons unsalted butter*
1   *tablespoon fresh lime juice*
Salt
Cayenne pepper

SALSA CRUDA:

4   *beefsteak tomatoes, diced*
6   *green onions, white part only, sliced*
4   *radishes, thinly sliced*
1   *Thai chile, finely chopped*
¼   *cup lime juice*
½   *cup extra-virgin olive oil*
1   *tablespoon chopped cilantro leaves*
1   *teaspoon chopped mint leaves*
1   *tablespoon chopped basil leaves*
1   *teaspoon kosher salt*

GROUPER:

6   *7-ounce skinless grouper fillets*
Vegetable oil, for rubbing
Salt
Cayenne pepper
3   *tablespoons unsalted butter, softened*

Preheat the oven to 350° F.

Place a 9- or 10-inch cast-iron skillet in the oven to heat. Using a box grater, coarsely grate the corn into a bowl, reserving all of the solids and juices. Add the oil to the hot skillet and swirl to coat. Spread the corn and juices in the skillet and bake for 45 minutes, until browned and crusty on the bottom. Scrape the corn into a sauce pan and stir in the butter and lime juice. Season with salt and cayenne; keep warm.

Prepare the Salsa Cruda by mixing all ingredients in a bowl. Let the salsa rest for at least ten minutes for the flavors to blend.

Reduce the oven temperature to 325° F. Heat a grill pan on a stove over high heat. Rub the grouper with oil and season with salt and cayenne. Grill fillets, still over high heat, skinned side up, until lightly charred, 2 to 3 minutes. Turn and transfer to a large baking sheet. Top each fillet with ½ tablespoon of butter and bake for about 3 minutes in the oven, until cooked through. Spoon the corn into small bowls. Plate the grouper fillets with any pan juices. Serve right away topped with the salsa. Serves 6.

3   tablespoons salted butter
5   tablespoons all-purpose flour
1   tablespoon vegetable oil
2   (1 ½-pound) boneless goose breast halves
     with skin, skin scored in a crosshatch pattern
2   (1 ½-pound) goose legs
7   ounces diced andouille sausage
4   cloves garlic, minced
2   celery ribs, finely diced
4   jalapeños, finely diced
1   large Spanish onion, finely diced
1   green bell pepper, finely diced
1   bay leaf
1   teaspoon each of chopped oregano, thyme,
     and sweet paprika
½   teaspoon cayenne pepper
½   cup dry Riesling
3   cups low-sodium chicken broth
3   cups water
4   large scallions, thinly sliced
2   tablespoons chopped parsley
Salt and freshly ground black pepper

In a small skillet, melt the butter. Stir in the flour and cook over moderately low heat, stirring often, until the mixture turns a rich, dark brown, about an hour and a half. Transfer the roux to a bowl and refrigerate until cold.

Meanwhile, in a large skillet, heat the oil. Add the goose breasts, skin side down, and cook over moderately high heat until browned, about 7 minutes. Pour off the fat, reserving 2 tablespoons. Turn the breasts and brown the other side for 3 minutes. Transfer to a rimmed baking sheet. Repeat with the goose legs, without reserving the fat.

In a large enameled cast-iron casserole, heat the reserved 2 tablespoons of goose fat. Add the andouille sausage, garlic, celery, jalapeños, onion, and bell pepper, and cook over moderate heat, stirring, until the vegetables are softened, about 10 minutes. Add the bay leaf, oregano, thyme, paprika, and cayenne, and cook, stirring, for 4 minutes. Add the wine and boil until reduced by half, for about 2 minutes. Add the broth and water, and bring to a boil. Add the goose parts and simmer over low heat, skimming occasionally, until the goose is tender, about an hour and a half. Transfer the goose to the baking sheet and let cool to room temperature. Discard the skin and bones and cut the meat into bite-size pieces.

Whisk 1 cup of the hot gumbo liquid into the cold roux. Whisk this mixture into the rest of the gumbo and bring to a simmer, stirring often. Simmer the gumbo over low heat for 15 minutes, stirring occasionally. Return the goose meat to the gumbo and bring to a simmer. Add the scallions and parsley, season with salt and black pepper, and serve. Serves 4.

CHILLED WATERMELON GAZPACHO WITH LUMP BLUE CRAB AND THAI BASIL

1   5- to 6-pound seedless red watermelon, rind removed
1   pound red bell peppers, seeded and stemmed
1   Thai chile, chopped
1 ¼ pound cucumbers, peeled and chopped
1   pound cherry tomatoes
4   teaspoons salt
White pepper to taste
¼   cup red wine vinegar
1   pound fresh Thai basil
½   cup grapeseed oil
¼   cup minced watermelon
¼   cup minced cucumber
¼   cup minced red onion
½   cup lump crabmeat

Using a food processor, puree the watermelon, red peppers, chile, and cucumbers. Strain the mixture and season with the salt, white pepper, and vinegar.

Blanche the basil in boiling salted water for 3 to 4 minutes, then shock it in ice water to stop the cooking. Squeeze out all the water you can, then roughly chop. Process it with the grapeseed oil to form a smooth puree. Strain out anything solid, leaving only the green basil oil.

In individual soup bowls, arrange small mounds of minced watermelon, cucumber, and red onion on the bottom. Also place lumps of crabmeat on the bottom and "connect the dots" of crabmeat with the basil oil. Serve the gazpacho chilled for adding to the bowl at table. Serves 6 to 8.

2   celery ribs, diced (about 1 cup)
1   large fennel bulb, diced
1   large onion, diced
3   cloves garlic, divided
10   country-style bone-in pork ribs
3   tablespoons grapeseed oil, divided
Salt and freshly ground pepper
½   cup fennel seeds, coarsely ground in a spice grinder
¼   cup pinenuts, toasted
1   jalapeño pepper, roasted, skinned, seeded, and chopped
1   cup loosely packed flat-leaf parsley
1   cup loosely packed basil leaves
1   large shallot, minced (about 2 tablespoons)
¼   cup grated Pecorino cheese
½   cup extra-virgin olive oil
1   tablespoon finely grated lemon zest

Preheat the oven to 375° F.

Combine the celery, fennel, onion, and two of the garlic cloves on a rimmed baking sheet. Place a wire rack over the vegetables, and set the baking sheet aside. Rub the ribs with 2 tablespoons of the grapeseed oil and season liberally with salt, pepper, and ground fennel seed.

Heat the remaining one tablespoon of grapeseed oil in a large skillet until the oil just begins to shimmer. Working in batches, cook the ribs over medium-high heat until golden brown, about 2 minutes, then turn the ribs over and cook until the other side is brown, another 1 to 2 minutes longer. Arrange the ribs in a single layer on the prepared baking sheet, transfer to the oven and roast until cooked through, about 35 to 40 minutes.

While ribs are baking, make the pesto: Place the pinenuts, jalapeño, parsley, basil, shallot, Pecorino, and the remaining garlic clove in the bowl of a food processor. Pulse until a smooth paste forms. With the processor running, slowly add the olive oil through the feed chute. Season the pesto with salt, pepper, and lemon zest, then transfer to a serving bowl.

To serve, arrange the roasted vegetables on a platter. Top with the ribs and serve with the jalapeño pesto on the side. Serves 4 to 6.

fearing's

fearing's

▼▼▼▼▼▼▼▼▼▼▼▼▼▼

"WE GREW UP AS LOBBY RATS AT THE HOLIDAY INN," offers superstar chef Dean Fearing by way of explanation, sitting among the seven "atmospheres" of his restaurant at a considerably more elegant hotel, the Ritz-Carlton Dallas. "We had the best time in the whole world—until my dad decided we had to start working."

Dean has been working, more or less, ever since, dividing his time between trying to become a rock star and doing his generation's historically unprecedented next best thing, becoming a celebrity chef. He still plays music, appearing at live gigs and even making a CD with his chef-heavy band, the Barb Wires. Still, in what has to qualify as his day job, Fearing has successfully closed out a full 25 years as the media darling of the Mansion on Turtle Creek to carve out his own place with his own name over the door at the Ritz-Carlton. In other words, he's still something of a "lobby rat." He's simply doing it in a much nicer lobby.

Dean was born in Ashland, Kentucky, on the Ohio River, and he still speaks with a friendly, Southern-ized brogue that can pass for a Texas accent, especially for those who notice his rattlesnake boots. But his upbringing was anything but entirely one place or another, since his father worked for Holiday Inn (then in its first great phase, as America discovered the driving vacation and the new interstate highway system).

"We lived in every city in the Midwest," Dean says today, and when he says "lived," he means at the local Holiday Inn. His father's job as troubleshooter, sent in to "fix" under-performing properties, meant the family slept in a guest room at the hotel and took virtually all their meals in the hotel dining room, coffee shop, café, or whatever the place had that passed for food and beverage. That was Dean's childhood home, one whose transient nature didn't seem to hinder his ability to form big dreams—most of them involving guitars you could plug in.

Traveling the Holiday Inn circuit year after year with his older brother and younger sister, Dean saw himself forming a band with his brother—like the Everly Brothers, perhaps—and turning out hits and becoming millionaires. They were working toward that when Dad, in his infinite wisdom, decided the two rockers-to-be had better start helping out in the Holiday Inn kitchen that kept the family fed, in every sense of the word.

"I was in the ninth grade, and we worked in the restaurant every afternoon and evening after school," Dean recalls, painfully aware that any time spent pulling meatloaf out of some oven was time not making girls squeal from the stage of some bar or club. "I hated every minute of it—until payday. Suddenly, my brother and I had a car, because we could buy one. We had a stereo. We became very popular with our friends. And, of course, we had guitars."

Cooking was hardly a *career* to the young Fearings; it was just something their father was making them do at first and then something that kept them in money till their big music dream came true, as it surely was going to. "Well," laughs Dean, "I guess we thought fame and fortune would happen a lot sooner, even though my parents kept saying we'd just be bums."

"I was in the ninth grade, and we worked in the restaurant every afternoon and evening after school," Dean recalls.

When adolescence and even college had faded away (Dean's single year at Ball State not producing much by way of guidance, perhaps because he didn't want any), he and his brother moved from the family's then-home in Louisville to play music in the heady college town of Columbia, Missouri, which for all its youth and energy was still a far cry from the revolutionary academic hotbeds on either coast. Even in open rebellion, it seems, Dean was picking up more and more of the middle-American work ethic. "We were just cooking to pay bills," he says. "It was the best two years of our lives."

At some point in 1974, the boys' father called them home, insisting he had arranged a government loan to open their own restaurant, to be called Fearing's. The brothers would run the kitchen, and they would take care of the front of the house, a mom-and-pop (and sons) restaurant, in the totally non-corporate, entrepreneurial American tradition. After all, they knew, even America's most successful hospitality brands (places like Holiday Inn, and especially like Hilton and Marriott) had started as little cafés somewhere, usually in the middle of nowhere. Sadly, at least sadly at the time, the loan failed to materialize and the Fearing boys were stranded at the Holiday Inn. Dean was ready to bail on the whole cooking thing, to roll the dice completely on his music, when his father insisted he first go talk to somebody at Jefferson (County) Community College. It was a man named Harvey Colgin, a retired corporate chef for Hilton in the South Pacific, who ended up changing Dean's life.

"I go down to see this guy for my dad, and I'm thinking, this'll take like three minutes," he recalls. "I come into the kitchen and there is this little man who is the epitome of the French chef, and I hand him my resume, and I think, OK, maybe *one* minute. So he looks up from the paper and asks, 'Do you know how to sauté?' I was like, 'Excuse me?' 'Do you know how to baste?' 'Uh, no.' He goes through this whole list, and then he says, 'Look, I can teach you these things.'" Dean pauses his story for a breath, just long enough to smile. "This guy is like the real deal, with his apprentice certificate from the Ritz Hotel in London, signed by Auguste Escoffier himself. I was enthralled. I stayed for two years. Really, I don't know how many apprentices to apprentices to Escoffier there are cooking today."

At Colgin's urging, Dean moved on from the community college to the Culinary Institute of America in Hyde Park, New York, and then from there to five years at a groundbreaking restaurant in Cincinnati called the Maisonette. As Dean recalls, it was the first place of its kind in America to pick up five stars from Mobil for its mix of French, Italian, and Continental fare. "Nothing else was on the radar," Dean says. "We were the

"Really, I don't know how many apprentices to apprentices to Escoffier there are cooking today."

first restaurant in the United States that brought fish from the Paris market on an overnight plane. That was as modern as modern could be."

It was Dean's next opportunity that accomplished something pivotal. The Pyramid Room at the Fairmont Hotel, which ended up figuring in the culinary evolution from French cooking toward something with a Texas personality, invited him to come work in Dallas.

"I fell in love with Dallas, with the energy of the city," he remembers. "I fell in love with the people here. And I fell in love with The Pyramid Room." Though the Room presumably loved him right back, it had a traditional kitchen run by "French boys who are never going to leave." So when Dean heard about Caroline Rose Hunt's plans to create the Mansion on Turtle Creek, the chance at upward mobility alone was enough to send him forth with resume. He started there as the saucier in 1980 and rose to executive sous chef the next year, running the Mansion's kitchen at night.

All in all, with a two-year break to operate his own place called Agnew's (named not after Richard Nixon's vice president but after business partner Tom Agnew, a former captain at the Mansion), Dean logged a quarter-century looking out over Turtle Creek. When he did return to the luxury hotel, after the recession killed off Agnew's, it was in the top chef's job.

Today, with his focus solidly on Fearing's at the Ritz-Carlton, Dean doesn't spend a lot of time dwelling on his years at the Mansion, except to say, "It was an unbelievable ride." Under his guidance, the restaurant there (known only by the hotel's name) moved to the forefront of the New American Cuisine movement as it exploded out from northern California to become New Southwestern, or even New Texas. Dean came to be recognized not only for unbelievable food and a new breed of service but as a kind of revolutionary, a visionary. In this, he often shared the stage with Chef Robert Del Grande of Café Annie down in Houston. And he still does share that stage since Robert has been a guitar-strumming member of the Barb Wires from the band's beginnings.

By the time Dean's business partner mentioned the possibility of opening another restaurant in another hotel, the chef had had about enough. Anyone familiar with the industry through this period knows that "corporate" (a four-letter word in every chef's vocabulary, which typically features enough of them already) had wrestled more and more control over individual hotels and their restaurants. So Dean said "thanks but no thanks" to his partner. Whatever he did next, he felt, it would be freestanding and, intrinsically, free-spirited. It wouldn't, insisted the chef who'd grown up in Holiday Inns, be in *any* hotel.

All that changed when the Ritz deal came together, a kind of hybrid in which Dean could and *would* be his own boss with "creative control" over everything from design to menu but—with a "license" rather than a "lease"—enjoy the full support of Ritz-Carlton's infrastructure. He built a space made of seven quite different spaces, some indoors and some outdoors, some fancy and some casual, all tied together under 18-foot ceilings with huge windows, oak, and Hill Country stone. In the loudest and liveliest of these dining areas, strewn about the open work area known as Dean's Kitchen, you hear the distinct echoes of the boss in the nightly soundtrack. Beatles, Rolling Stones, Tommy James, The Kinks, Jimi Hendrix—all their best rock stuff, too, not some B-side ballads. It's as though Dean gets to be onstage now in more ways than one, without even lugging any of his vintage guitars to work.

"All my employees are Ritz employees," he explains. "We have use of their laundry, human resources, engineering. I'm the only one who's not a Ritz employee." Dean grins, a "lobby rat" who grew up to be Theseus, finding his way out of the Minotaur's dark labyrinth. "It's the best of all worlds," he says.

> "I fell in love with Dallas, with the energy of the city. I fell in love with the people here. And I fell in love with The Pyramid Room."

GRIDDLED SEA SCALLOPS WITH SHREDDED SHORT RIBS

ON FOIE GRAS—SWEET POTATO PUREE AND ROYAL TRUMPET MUSHROOM RAGOUT

Salt and pepper to taste
16 *(U-10 size) sea scallops, cleaned*
4 *tablespoons olive oil*
2 *shallots, diced*
3 *cloves garlic, minced*
½ *pound Royal Trumpet mushrooms, cleaned and thinly sliced*
1 *cup julienned carrots*
½ *pound braised short rib (recipe to follow)*
1 *cup baby mustard greens, or any bitter salad greens*
2 *cups sweet potato-foie gras puree (recipe to follow)*
½ *cup horseradish cream (recipe to follow)*

Season scallops with salt and pepper. In a medium sauce pan over high heat, heat 2 tablespoons of oil and then add the scallops. Cook for about 1 minute on each side until golden brown. Separately, in a medium-size sauté pan over medium-high heat, add the remaining 2 tablespoons of oil and add the shallot, garlic, sliced mushrooms, carrots, and the braised short ribs. Sauté for 2 minutes, stirring constantly. Add the greens, toss together, season with salt and pepper to taste, and remove from the heat.

On four warm plates, place a large tablespoon of the sweet potato-foie gras puree in the center. Spoon equal amounts of the sautéed vegetables and short ribs over the puree and place four of the scallops on top. To garnish the plate, place a tablespoon of the horseradish cream on the side.

SWEET POTATO – FOIE GRAS PUREE:
6 *ounces foie gras (scrap and end pieces can be used)*
2 *sweet potatoes, peeled and chopped*
2 *carrots, peeled and medium-diced*
2 *shallots, sliced*
4 *cloves garlic*
2 *cups dry white wine*
2 *cups heavy cream*
4 *sprigs thyme, stems removed*
Salt and pepper to taste
Sherry vinegar to taste

In a medium-size sauce pan, cook the foie gras over medium heat and slowly render out much of the fat. Add the sweet potatoes, carrots, shallots, and garlic. Continue cooking, stirring regularly, for 20 minutes. Add the white wine, reduce by half. Add cream and thyme, and reduce by half. Check doneness of the vegetables; they should be soft all the way through. Puree in a blender, and season with salt, pepper, and sherry vinegar to taste.

DR PEPPER BRAISED SHORT RIBS:
2   pounds beef short ribs
¼   cup chopped celery
¼   cup chopped carrot
¼   cup chopped onion
1   sprig thyme
1   teaspoon ground sage
1   bay leaf
2   ancho chiles, seeds and stems removed
½   teaspoon ground cumin
½   teaspoon ground coriander
1   teaspoon smoked paprika
¼   cup red wine
1   teaspoon rough-cut jalapeño pepper
¼   cup chopped tomato
1   quart Dublin Dr Pepper
2   quarts chicken stock
Salt and pepper to taste

Preheat the oven to 300° F.

In a large sauté pan over medium-high heat, season and sear short ribs, fat side down. After 3 minutes, turn the short ribs over and cook for an additional 3 minutes. Remove the short ribs from the pan and set aside. Add the celery, carrot, and onion to the pan and cook until golden brown, approximately 5 minutes. Add the spices, jalapeño, and tomato and continue to cook for an additional 5 minutes. Next add the red wine and reduce the liquid by half. Add the Dr Pepper and reduce by half. Add chicken stock, season, and add the short ribs back to the pan. Cover with foil and place in the oven for 4 to 5 hours, until tender. Remove the short ribs from the oven and set aside. Cut the ribs into 1-inch pieces. Strain the remaining liquid from the pan through a fine mesh strainer and save for future use.

HORSERADISH CREAM:
½   cup sour cream
2   tablespoons prepared horseradish
1   teaspoon finely chopped dill pickle
Lemon juice to taste
Salt and pepper to taste

In a medium-size mixing bowl, stir together all of the ingredients, adjusting flavor with lemon juice. Season with salt and pepper to taste. Serves 4.

LOBSTER COCONUT BISQUE WITH SIZZLING RICE

COCONUT BISQUE:

2	tablespoons vegetable oil
1	large yellow onion, chopped
2	cloves garlic, chopped
1	tablespoon ginger root, peeled and chopped
1	stalk lemongrass
1	stalk celery, chopped
1	quart lobster stock
1	quart coconut milk
1	cup cooked white rice
1	packet Tom Ka paste
2	kaffir lime leaves
½	teaspoon fish sauce

Salt and pepper to taste
Lime juice to taste
Sizzling rice (recipe to follow)

1	bunch cilantro, chopped

Heat oil in a large pot over medium-high heat and add the onion, garlic, ginger, lemongrass, and celery. Sauté for 5 minutes, then add the lobster stock and the coconut milk. Bring to a boil and add the cooked white rice. Lower the bisque to a simmer, and cook for 15 minutes while continuously stirring to prevent scorching. Remove the soup from the heat and puree in a blender for a smooth texture.

Strain the bisque back into the pot and simmer over medium heat with the Tom Ka paste, kaffir lime leaves, and fish sauce for another 15 minutes. Remove from the heat and season to taste with salt, pepper, and fresh lime juice. Before serving, remove the kaffir lime leaves. In each warm soup bowl, evenly distribute the sizzling rice and 6 ounces of coconut bisque into each bowl. Garnish with chopped cilantro.

SIZZLING RICE:

2   cups medium-grain rice
2   tablespoons seasoned rice vinegar
2   tablespoons olive oil, divided
½   cup diced yellow onion
1   tablespoon minced garlic
1   tablespoon minced ginger root
½   cup diced carrots
¼   cup diced red bell pepper
¼   cup diced yellow bell pepper
¼   cup shelled fresh English peas
1   tablespoon soy sauce

Measure two cups of plain, medium-grain rice into a pot. Pour 2½ cups of cold water into the pot. Place the pot over a moderate to high heat. Turn down the heat to the minimum possible once the rice comes to a rolling boil and continue heating for 5 more minutes. Place a well-sealed lid on the pot. Turn off the heat after 5 minutes. Do not lift the lid: It is important to leave the steam inside to cook the rice through. The pot of rice will be fully cooked after about 10 minutes. Pour the rice out onto a sheet pan in a single layer. Using a fork, break the rice apart while sprinkling the seasoned rice vinegar throughout. Allow the rice to cool.

Heat a large heavy-bottomed skillet over medium-high heat. When hot, add 1 tablespoon of the oil. Add the onions to the pan, season with salt and pepper, and cook for 1 to 2 minutes. Add the garlic and ginger, and stir-fry until fragrant, about 30 seconds. Add the carrots, bell peppers, and peas. Cook for approximately 2 minutes. Transfer contents of the skillet to a large bowl.

Return the pan to the heat and add 1 tablespoon of oil. Add the rice to the pan and use a spoon to break up any clumps. Stir-fry the rice for 2 minutes. Add the soy sauce to combine with the rice. Stop stirring and let the rice cook undisturbed until it gets slightly crispy, about 2 minutes. Stir the rice again, breaking up any new clumps. Add the vegetables and stir-fry all the ingredients together, adjusting the seasoning with salt and pepper if necessary. Serves 6.

MAPLE–BLACK PEPPERCORN–SOAKED BUFFALO TENDERLOIN

ON ANSON MILLS JALAPEÑO GRITS
WITH CRISPY BUTTERNUT SQUASH TAQUITO

1   cup maple syrup
2   tablespoons freshly cracked black pepper
2   cloves garlic, peeled and finely chopped
1   large shallot, peeled and finely chopped
1   teaspoon finely chopped fresh sage
1   teaspoon finely chopped fresh thyme
Crushed red pepper flakes to taste
1   (24-ounce) whole buffalo tenderloin, trimmed of
    all fat and silver skin
Salt and black pepper to taste
2   tablespoons vegetable oil
jalapeño grits (recipe to follow)
tangle of greens (recipe to follow)
4   butternut squash taquitos (recipe to follow)
Yellow tomato pico de gallo (recipe to follow)
Smoked chili aioli (recipe to follow)
4   sprigs fresh cilantro

In a small bowl, combine maple, black pepper, garlic, shallot, sage, thyme, and pepper flakes. Stir to combine, and add fillets. Let the buffalo tenderloin marinate in the maple mixture for 8 hours or overnight, rotating the tenderloin every 2 hours.

Remove the tenderloin from the mixture and cut into 6-ounce steaks. Season with salt and pepper. Heat oil in a large cast-iron skillet over medium-high heat. When hot, lay buffalo in skillet and brown for 4 minutes. Turn and brown for an additional 3 minutes or until desired degree of doneness is reached.

JALAPEÑO GRITS:
1   tablespoon olive oil
1   small onion, diced
1   teaspoon minced garlic
1   tablespoon minced jalapeño
1   teaspoon chopped fresh thyme
6   cups chicken stock
2   cups Anson Mills white grits
1   teaspoon smoked paprika
½   ounce Tabasco pepper sauce

In a large sauce pan (grits will expand in volume during the cooking), over medium-high heat, sauté oil and onions for 2 minutes or until translucent. Add the garlic, jalapeño, and thyme. Add chicken stock, and bring to a boil. Sprinkle in the grits a handful at a time, stirring constantly. Reduce the heat to a simmer, and cook the grits about 25 minutes, until they are thickened and soft in texture. Stir the grits occasionally as they cook. Add the smoked paprika and Tabasco. Season with salt and pepper to taste.

TANGLE OF GREENS:
2   tablespoons olive oil
1   tablespoon minced shallots
1   teaspoon minced garlic
2   cups packed, washed stemless spinach
1   cup packed, washed arugula leaves
Salt and pepper to taste

In a large sauté pan over medium-high heat, add the oil, shallots, and garlic, and sauté for 1 minute. Add the greens and continue to cook, stirring constantly, until the greens have wilted. Season with salt and pepper.

YELLOW TOMATO PICO DE GALLO:
1   large yellow tomato, seeded and finely diced
1   small jalapeño, seeded and finely diced
1   small shallot, finely diced
Juice of 1 lime
Salt and pepper to taste

In a small mixing bowl, combine all of the ingredients.

BUTTERNUT SQUASH TAQUITO:
1   pound butternut squash
2   cups vegetable oil
1   sprig rosemary
1   tablespoon minced shallot
½   tablespoon minced garlic
¼   cup Cotija cheese
4   corn tortillas

Preheat the oven to 350° F.

Cut squash in half and remove seeds. Rub the squash with 1 teaspoon of the vegetable oil and season with salt and pepper. Place a sprig of rosemary in the cavity of the squash. Turn the squash over with skin facing up on a sheet pan and roast until tender, about 30 minutes. Remove from oven and let cool. Scoop out the squash from the skin using a spoon. Place the squash into a food processor and pulse 3 to 4 times until evenly chopped. Remove the squash and place into a mixing bowl. In a medium-size sauté pan over medium-high heat, sweat the shallot and garlic for about 2 minutes. Remove from the heat and fold into the squash with the cheese.

Warm the corn tortillas to make them pliable. Place two ounces of mix on each corn tortilla; roll up, then skewer with a toothpick so that they stay together. Heat the remainder of the vegetable oil to 350° F and deep-fry the taquito for 4 minutes, or until crisp. Remove the taquito from the heat and drain on a paper towel.

SMOKED CHILI AIOLI:
1   large egg yolk
5   cloves smoked garlic
1   smoked red bell pepper, seeds removed
2   smoked shallots, minced
2   anchovy fillets
2   tablespoons Dijon mustard
1   tablespoon Worcestershire sauce
½   teaspoon Sriracha sauce
2   teaspoons sherry vinegar
1   teaspoon smoked paprika
¾   cup grapeseed oil
¾   cup olive oil
2   red jalapeños, roasted and chopped
1   tablespoon cilantro, chopped
2   tablespoons lime juice
Salt to taste

In blender, combine egg yolks, garlic, red bell pepper, shallots, anchovies, mustard, Worcestershire, chili sauce, sherry vinegar, and paprika. Puree until smooth. Slowly add oils until dressing is emulsified and creamy. Add chopped jalapeños, cilantro, lime juice, and salt to taste.

To serve, start with jalapeño grits in the middle of each plate. Cut each tenderloin on the bias through the middle and crisscross on top of the grits. Place an evenly portioned tangle of greens at the back side of the buffalo. Lay the butternut squash taquito between the buffalo and the tangle of greens and sprinkle with pico de gallo. On the front side of the buffalo, spoon a pool of smoked chili aioli. Garnish with cilantro and serve. Serves 4.

BUTTERSCOTCH CUSTARD WITH CARAMELIZED APPLE FRITTERS

BUTTERSCOTCH CUSTARD:

1 ½	teaspoons gelatin powder		½	cup sour cream
2	tablespoons cold water		¼	cup unsalted butter
1 ½	cups heavy cream		1	whole vanilla bean, split and scraped
3	ounces cream cheese		⅛	teaspoon salt
½	cup dark brown sugar		2	tablespoons Cragganmore scotch

Pour water over the gelatin powder and set aside. Over a double boiler, melt the heavy cream, cream cheese, sugar, sour cream, butter, vanilla bean, and salt; whisk until smooth. Add the gelatin and scotch to the cream mixture. Strain the mixture and pour into six 4- or 5-ounce glasses. Place in refrigerator until set.

CARAMELIZED APPLES:

½ cup granulated sugar
2 apples, peeled and small-diced
½ teaspoon cinnamon

FRITTER BATTER:

1 ½	cups all-purpose flour		2	eggs, separated
¼	cup granulated sugar		2	teaspoons melted unsalted butter
1	teaspoon cinnamon		½	cup whole milk
1	whole vanilla bean, split and scraped			Cinnamon-sugar
½	teaspoon lemon zest			Caramel sauce

Pour the sugar in a medium sauce pan and caramelize over medium heat. Slowly add the diced apples and cinnamon; cook until tender and all of the sugar is dissolved. The liquid will be dark brown. Set aside to cool. After apples have cooled down, strain and set aside for fritter batter.

Preheat the oven to 350° F.

In a bowl, combine the flour, sugar, cinnamon, vanilla bean, and lemon zest, and set aside. In another bowl, combine the egg yolks, melted butter, and milk. Slowly add the liquid ingredients to the dry ingredients, whisking constantly, avoiding lumps. Whip the egg whites to a hard peak and fold into batter. Fold the strained apples into the batter. Use a ¾-ounce ice cream scoop or a spoon to deep-fry the fritters. Fry until dark brown and roll in cinnamon-sugar. Top with caramel sauce. Serve three fritters per plate, with custard and ice cream, preferably pecan-toffee flavor. Serves 6.

CHOCOLATE CAKE:

15	ounces granulated sugar		2	whole eggs
8	ounces all-purpose flour		2	egg yolks
4	ounces cocoa powder		¾	teaspoon vanilla paste
1 ½	teaspoons salt		1	cup buttermilk
1	teaspoon baking powder		1	cup coffee
2	teaspoons baking soda		2	ounces melted unsalted butter

Preheat the oven to 325° F.

In a mixer, combine sugar, flour, cocoa, salt, baking powder, and baking soda. Add the eggs, yolks, vanilla, and half of the buttermilk. Mix on medium speed until combined, and scrape the bowl. On low speed, gradually add the remaining buttermilk, coffee, and butter. Scrape well after each addition. In a sprayed muffin tin, or in foil containers, fill halfway with chocolate cake batter. Bake for about 15 minutes, until toothpick inserted in center comes out dry. Remove from the oven and with skewers or toothpicks, poke holes in the top of the cakes. Pour caramel sauce (see recipe) over each cake.

CARAMEL SAUCE:
14 ounces granulated sugar
2 ounces water
5 ¼ ounces light corn syrup
5 ounces unsalted butter
9 ¾ ounces heavy cream
½ teaspoon salt
½ vanilla bean, scraped

Combine sugar and water in a sauce pan. Heat until sugar begins to caramelize, swirling the pan (do not stir). Cook until very dark, about 5 to 7 minutes. Add the corn syrup, butter, and cream. Whisk until smooth. Remove from heat and add salt and vanilla. Serves 20.

stephan pyles | samar

IT'S HARD TO TELL WHICH MAKES STEPHAN PYLES MORE OF A TEXAN—growing up as a fifth-generation denizen of the Lone Star State or having parents who ran a truck stop.

For the record, the first is something Stephan reports matter-of-factly, like the operating dates of his landmark Dallas restaurants Routh Street Cafe, Baby Routh, and Star Canyon or his current fine-dining destination called, simply, Stephan Pyles. The second, however, unleashes a multimedia barrage of memories. Had Marcel Proust been born in Amarillo instead of Auteuil, he'd be dang proud.

"It wasn't the end of the earth," Stephan remembers of his West Texas hometown of Big Spring. He pauses, a comedian with admirable timing. "But you could *see* it from there." No matter how fancy the dining room in his namesake eatery, you can also see that Stephan keeps at least one foot in his own past. "Big Spring had the last inland refinery. I thought the entire world smelled like that. I was pleased that it didn't.

"At our café, there was always that sense of nourishment and hospitality and service to people. There was always food and singing, always Tammy and Waylon on the jukebox and always those beehive hairdos on the waitresses. I never could separate any of that from the restaurant, and it was always an extension of home to me. In those days," Stephan laughs, coming back with reluctance to the world of international food celebrity, "the chef was just a guy with a floppy hat and a cigarette in his mouth, all bent over a deep-fryer."

Stephan was only ten when he started "working" at the café, though his parents and all those waitresses insisted he was only "playing." It would be several more years before he understood what restaurant work really *felt* like. But the ritual of being the cute little kid bussing tables gave him a lifetime of warmth around subjects like family, camaraderie, and teamwork, qualities that every restaurant that functions well counts on to get it through the night.

By the time he was ready for college, Stephan entertained some idea of being a public school music teacher; between the melodies on the jukebox at the café and the others he heard at church on Sunday, he had a decent-enough grounding. He studied music at East Texas State, which later became a satellite of Texas A&M. "I'm an Aggie by proxy," he laughs. Still, once he'd graduated and it was time to actually teach somebody, he got clear in a hurry on only one subject: He wanted to do almost anything but that.

As it has for so many young Americans hoping to replace what they *don't* want with what they *do*, a summer of backpacking around Europe with his best friend gave Stephan a fateful respite. This was hardly today's notion of culinary travel with visits to wineries and farmers' markets interspersed with meals in Michelin three-star restaurants. It was simply budget youth sightseeing. Yet of necessity, it did involve rounding up meals. And in Europe, in everyday sections of major cities as well as in tiny villages, rounding up meals can prove a revelation.

"What was most influential," Stephan remembers, "were the neighborhoods with this amazing dedication to

"What was most influential, were the neighborhoods with this amazing dedication to seasonality and freshness."

seasonality and freshness. There were no grocery stores. It was an absolutely new way of thinking for me."

Within days of his return to Texas, the young man had tossed aside all remaining notions of teaching music for a new vision of life in food and wine. Despite limited appreciation for what a chef was or even did, Stephan decided he wanted to—no, he *had* to—become one, and he embarked upon two years of doing odd jobs around any restaurant he could talk his way into. Additionally, he spent time working as a waiter and a bartender, vaguely convinced that somewhere in his future these non-kitchen skills might come in handy.

Somewhere along the way, one of Stephan's restaurant friends ended up cooking at the Waldorf-Astoria in New York, and that friend ended up talking to some high-end caterers who were organizing a new upscale cooking school at the Robert Mondavi Winery in Napa Valley. These caterers asked who might be good to bring onboard and that friend—a friend indeed—suggested Stephan Pyles down in Texas. A page was turning, even if Stephan didn't know it yet. Those memories of his parents' truck stop were about to be overwhelmed with another vision of cooking altogether.

The Mondavi program, pairing wine tastings and cooking classes with household-name culinarians, was called the Great Chefs of France Cooking School. And that's exactly what it turned out to be. The first classes Stephan worked on starred Robert Mondavi's dear friend Julia Child and also Simone Beck, who had helped Julia write her first great magnum opus, *Mastering the Art of French Cooking*. That was May of 1981. After that, it was one unbroken stream of three-star chefs.

"I was star-struck," Stephan remembers of his encounters with famous chef after famous chef. "I wanted to *be* them, I wanted their products, I wanted everything they had. And I slowly came to think: This is something that's missing here in America. Before long I was asking: Why can't we take the techniques, the concepts of French cuisine, and do something that's American?"

It's worth noting that Stephan was in northern California when he was thinking and asking these things, arguably the first region in the country to start experimenting with that very notion. Chefs like Alice Waters of Chez Panisse and Jeremiah Tower, first at Chez Panisse and later at his own Stars, were digging through the produce grown in their neighborhoods, if not in their own backyard gardens, and applying French ideas to the art of making them wonderful. It was exactly what the best French chefs were doing in France, so it was hardly a

"Before long I was asking: Why can't we take the techniques, the concepts of French cuisine, and do something that's American?"

revolutionary notion. What *was* revolutionary was that they were doing it in America.

Most chefs joining the movement called what they were cooking New American Cuisine, and with the opening of Routh Street Cafe in Dallas in 1983, Stephan saw no reason to come up with something different. As he looks back now, there was not yet anything Texas or even Southwestern about the flavors he was turning out; it was simply the fact that everything allowed to enter his kitchen door was grown, raised, or prepared in the United States. Forget getting great things from Texas, Stephan remembers; fresh herbs, baby carrots, even red bell peppers all had to be flown in from California.

The success of Routh Street pushed Stephan forward to create the cleverly named Baby Routh. The original was simply turning too many diners away every night. Baby Routh was more casual, larger, more fun—and no one had more fun making it happen than the chef himself. He put even the restaurant's logo in multicolored child's handwriting, the menu in a school-style three-ring binder. Both Rouths were huge hits, attracting diners from all over north Texas—and food media from New York, Los Angeles, and even Europe. Seen in the context of the larger New American movement, what was happening on the plate in Dallas was a food story with global implications.

But it still wasn't Texas enough.

"My attention span seems to be ten years," Stephan jokes, remembering his decision to sell his business partner the two restaurants in Dallas along with two others they'd spun off in Minneapolis, of all places. "I wanted to do something more Texan. Of all the New Southwestern chefs who came out of that time, even the ones working here in Texas, I was the only actual Texan. And I could never do the kind of food or the kind of décor I wanted at Routh Street. It was much too refined."

Star Canyon, the answer to what must have been several hundred of Stephan's hopes and dreams, opened with 160 seats plus 40 more outside, in the early nineties. Everything about the place was big and bold like Texas, from the cowboy hats in the lights in the alcoves to the menu to the wine list. On the latter, only wines produced in Texas (by an industry that had barely gotten its feet on the ground then) were offered as "domestic." Wines from everywhere else in the world, including California, were listed as "imported." From signature dishes like the cowboy ribeye and the tamale tart (both still on the menu at Stephan Pyles) to a broad array of spicy spins on chili, tacos, tamales, and enchiladas, the menu at Star Canyon was the stuff of every Texan's food fantasies.

"This was my love song to Texas," Stephan says simply. "There was never any question where you were."

In the next ten years allotted by his "attention span," the chef and new business partners took Star Canyon through several iterations, spinning off four restaurants in all before selling the package to Carlson Worldwide

"I wanted to do something more Texan."

(best known for its TGIFriday's) based in, once again, Minneapolis. The idea then was to develop, with Stephan as the highly paid consulting chef, ten or fifteen Star Canyons in different large cities, plus a lot of smaller, more casual "Canyanitas" on top of that. Stephan had a five-year contract with Carlson. He lasted three.

"I have the mentality of a small business owner," he explains, touching his hand to the salt and pepper shakers on the table. "If this doesn't look right *here*, for instance, I want to move it *there*. I don't like having to call a corporate office to ask permission." Stephan ponders his entire career, going back to that truck stop in Big Spring. "When it comes to customers, you have to be able to turn on a dime."

Today, after traveling the world for five years doing restaurant consulting, Stephan is the Chef Who Came in from the Cold. Consulting was fine, he says, and paid more than well enough. But he needed a home. He needed his own song to sing, not just someone else's. And most of all, he needed his own stage on which to stand and sing it. The restaurant called Stephen Pyles is clearly that stage, but then again, so is the newer Samar, a couple blocks down the street in the heart of the Dallas Arts District.

Samar is Stephan's love song to the flavors of India, the Eastern Mediterranean, and Spain. If that taste combination makes no sense to you, then you missed the chapter on the spice routes, the Crusades, and the Moorish invasion of Andalusia. And probably something to do with Alexander the Great while you were at it.

"I don't have a plan," Stephan says, with a bit of hard-earned pride. "Over the years I've had three-year plans and five-year plans, and at the end of each period, it never looked at all like the plan. I have to have a platform. I have to be creative. And planning, opening, and running new restaurants—that mad chaos that frustrates so many people—that's what excites me. I've never opened a concept and said I'm going to have 100 of these. I've always said, Let's see if *one* works first. The only thing I do know is that it'll be exciting."

SALMON CEVICHE VERACRUZANA WITH CAPERS,

GREEN OLIVES, AND JALAPEÑOS

ROASTED TOMATO SALSA:

4   ripe tomatoes
1   yellow onion, peeled and cut into quarters
4   mashed garlic cloves
1   red bell pepper
2   jalapeños
Olive oil
Salt to taste

CEVICHE:

1   (10-ounce) salmon fillet, skin removed and
    meat cut into 1-by-¼-inch strips
2   tablespoons key lime juice
Salt to taste (about 2 teaspoons)
2   tablespoons drained capers
2   tablespoons chopped pitted green olives
1   tablespoon chopped cilantro
1   jalapeño, seeded and minced
¼   cup roasted tomato salsa

Preheat the oven to 450° F.

To make the roasted tomato salsa, toss all items with a small amount of olive oil, season with salt, and place on a baking sheet. Place in the oven and roast until tomatoes begin to blacken and peppers and onions are a deep brown color, about 20 to 30 minutes. Remove from the oven and let cool. Peel and de-seed the chiles and peppers. Place meat of peppers and all remaining items, including the juice on the baking sheet, into a blender and puree until smooth. Taste, adjust seasoning with salt, and taste again. Chill the salsa before mixing the ceviche.

To make the ceviche, place the salmon in a glass or stainless steel bowl and add the lime juice and salt. Let the ceviche marinate for 5 minutes. Add the remaining ingredients and mix well. Serves 4.

CUSTARD:

2	heads garlic, halved crosswise
2	tablespoons olive oil
3	cups heavy cream
4	egg yolks
2	teaspoons kosher salt
¼	teaspoon freshly ground white pepper

TART SHELL:

1	large red bell pepper, cored, seeded, and chopped
3	ancho chiles
2	cups masa harina
¼	cup yellow cornmeal
2	teaspoons ground cumin
2	teaspoons kosher salt
¼	teaspoon cayenne pepper
6	tablespoons vegetable shortening

CRAB TOPPING:

2	tablespoons olive oil
½	small yellow onion, finely chopped
¼	red bell pepper, cored, seeded, and finely chopped
¼	yellow bell pepper, cored, seeded, and finely chopped
¼	poblano chile, halved, seeded, and finely chopped
10	ounces fresh lump crabmeat, picked and cleaned
2	teaspoons fresh lime juice
2	tablespoons chopped cilantro

To make the custard, preheat the oven to 350° F. Place garlic in foil, drizzle with oil, and wrap tight; bake until soft, 35 to 40 minutes. Squeeze roasted garlic into a bowl. In a 4-quart sauce pan over medium heat, simmer cream, stirring, until reduced to about 1 cup, 25 to 30 minutes. Vigorously whisk reserved garlic into cream; let cool slightly. In a bowl, whisk egg yolks. Whisk in cream mixture, salt, and pepper. Cover custard with plastic wrap; let cool.

To make the tart shell, bring a 2-quart sauce pan of water to a boil. Add bell peppers; cook until soft, about 10 minutes. Drain peppers; transfer to a food processor and puree until smooth. Reserve ¾ cup pepper puree. Meanwhile, soften ancho chiles according to these steps. Transfer chiles to a food processor with ½ cup soaking water. Puree until smooth; strain through a sieve. Reserve 6 tablespoons of chile puree.

In a medium bowl, combine masa harina, cornmeal, cumin, salt, and cayenne; set aside. In a large bowl, beat shortening, using a handheld mixer, until fluffy. Sprinkle in dry ingredients and mix until pea-size crumbs form. Add reserved pepper and chile purees and mix (dough will be very sticky). Form dough into a flat disk; transfer to a 9-inch tart pan with a removable bottom. Press dough evenly over bottom and up the sides of the pan to a ¼-inch thickness. Pour in custard; cover with plastic wrap.

Place a bamboo steamer inside a wide-bottomed pot; pour in 1 inch of water. Bring to a boil, reduce to medium-low, and transfer tart to steamer. Cover and steam until custard is just set, about 25 minutes. Using kitchen towels, lift out tart. Remove plastic wrap and tart ring, and transfer tart to a platter.

To make the crab topping, heat oil in a 12-inch skillet over high heat. Add onions; cook until soft, 4 to 5 minutes. Add peppers, chiles, crab, and lime; cook until just hot. Stir in cilantro and season with salt. Spoon crab mixture over tart. Serves 8 to 10.

COWBOY RIBEYE WITH ONION RINGS

Steak:

¼ cup sweet paprika
3 tablespoons kosher salt
1 ½ tablespoons ground guajillo chile
1 ½ tablespoons ground pasilla chile
1 ½ tablespoons ground chipotle chile
1 ½ tablespoons sugar
4 (16-ounce) bone-in ribeye steaks

In a medium bowl, whisk together ¼ cup paprika, 2 tablespoons salt, guajillo, pasilla, and chipotle chiles, and sugar. Put steaks on a parchment-lined baking sheet; rub with the chile mixture. Refrigerate steaks overnight.

Onion Rings:

Canola oil, for frying
1 small yellow onion, cut crosswise into
  ⅛-inch-thick rings
1 cup whole milk
1 ½ cups flour
1 tablespoon chili powder
1 teaspoon cayenne pepper
½ teaspoon ground cumin
¼ teaspoon ground black pepper

Pour oil into a 4-quart sauce pan to a depth of 2 inches; heat over medium-high heat until a deep-fry thermometer reads 350° F. Meanwhile, put onions and milk into a bowl; let soak for 20 minutes. In a large bowl, whisk together the salt, flour, chili powder, cayenne, cumin, and pepper. Working in batches, remove onions from the milk, shake off excess, and toss in seasoned flour. Fry onions until crisp, about 3 minutes. Drain on paper towels; season with salt. Set aside.

Build a medium-hot fire with mesquite charcoal or heat a gas grill to medium-high. (Alternatively, heat a grill pan over medium-high heat.) Grill steaks, turning once, until medium rare, about 12 minutes. Serve with onion rings. Serves 4.

DRESSING:

1	teaspoon ground cumin
4	teaspoons Dijon mustard
2	tablespoons pureed roasted garlic
1	teaspoon tamarind paste
2	tablespoons chipotle chile puree
4	anchovy fillets
1	tablespoon balsamic vinegar
2	tablespoons fresh lemon juice
1	small shallot, minced
3	egg yolks
1	teaspoon pure red chile powder
⅔	cup extra-virgin olive oil
⅓	cup vegetable oil

Salt and cayenne pepper to taste

CROUTONS:

4	serrano chiles, seeded and minced
½	teaspoon cayenne pepper
1½	teaspoons salt
2¾	cups whole milk
1½	cups yellow cornmeal
1½	quarts peanut oil

SALAD:

2	heads red romaine lettuce, rinsed and dried
2	heads green romaine lettuce, rinsed and dried
4	ounces pecorino or Parmesan cheese, shaved

To prepare the dressing, place all the ingredients, except the oil and seasonings, in a blender, and blend until smooth. With the machine running, slowly drizzle in the oil and incorporate thoroughly. Season with salt and cayenne, and set aside.

To prepare the croutons, combine the serranos, cayenne, salt, and milk in a medium sauce pan, and bring to a rapid boil. Slowly add 1 cup of the cornmeal while stirring constantly. Cook over medium heat for 3 to 5 minutes, until the mixture pulls away from the sides of the pan and forms a ball. Press the mixture into a 9-inch pan lined with plastic wrap. Place in the refrigerator, uncovered, to cool about 30 minutes. Remove from the pan and dice into ½-inch cubes.

To prepare the salad greens, de-rib the inside leaves of each head of the romaine, and then tear the leaves into bite-sized pieces.

To finish the salad, heat the peanut oil to 350° F. Dredge the polenta cubes in the remaining ½ cup of cornmeal. Fry the croutons until crisp, about 1 to 2 minutes. Remove from the oil with a slotted spoon, drain on paper towels, and keep warm until use.

In a large salad bowl, toss the romaine with the dressing and half of the cheese. Divide the tossed greens evenly among eight plates and top with the remaining cheese and warm croutons. Serves 8.

HEAVEN AND HELL CAKE

GANACHE:

2   pounds milk chocolate, such as Valrhona, chopped
1 ½ cups heavy cream

ANGEL FOOD CAKE:

1 ½ cups confectioners' sugar
1   cup cake flour
1 ½ cups egg whites, about 10 eggs
1   teaspoon cream of tartar

⅛   teaspoon kosher salt
1   cup granulated sugar
2   teaspoons pure vanilla extract
1   teaspoon almond extract

DEVIL'S FOOD CAKE:

½   cup vegetable shortening, plus more for pan
1 ½ cups cake flour, plus more for pan
1   teaspoon baking soda
¾   teaspoon kosher salt
¼   teaspoon baking powder

1   cup coffee
½   cup cocoa powder, sifted
1 ½ cups granulated sugar
1   teaspoon pure vanilla extract
2   eggs

PEANUT BUTTER MOUSSE:

1 ½ pounds cream cheese, at room temperature
1   quart smooth peanut butter, at room temperature

3 ½ cups confectioners' sugar, sifted
1 ½ cups heavy cream

To prepare the ganache, place the chocolate in a medium-size bowl. Bring cream to a boil in a 2-quart sauce pan; pour cream over the chocolate and let sit to melt for 5 minutes. Using a rubber spatula, combine the chocolate and cream, stirring from the center outward. Cover with plastic wrap and set aside to let rest for 4 hours.

To prepare the angel food cake, heat the oven to 325° F. Line bottom of a 10-inch round cake pan with ungreased parchment paper. In a medium bowl, sift together confectioners' sugar and flour; set flour mixture aside. In a large bowl, beat egg whites, cream of tartar, and salt with a handheld mixer on low speed until frothy. Increase mixer speed to medium, sprinkle in sugar, vanilla, and almond extract, and beat until stiff peaks form. Sprinkle half of the confectioners' sugar–flour mixture over egg whites. Using a rubber spatula, fold until just combined. Repeat with remaining flour mixture. Pour batter into prepared cake pan and bake until top of cake springs back when touched, 45 to 50 minutes. Transfer cake to a rack and let cool.

To prepare the devil's food cake, heat oven to 350° F. Grease a 10-inch round cake pan with shortening and dust with flour to coat; shake out excess flour and set pan aside. In a medium bowl, whisk together cake flour, baking soda, salt, and baking powder; set flour mixture aside. In another medium bowl, whisk the coffee and cocoa powder until smooth. Set coffee mixture aside. In a large bowl, beat the shortening, sugar, vanilla, and eggs with a handheld mixer on medium speed until pale and fluffy, about 2 minutes. Alternately add the flour mixture and the coffee mixture to the bowl with the shortening mixture in three stages, beating to combine after each addition. Pour the batter into the prepared cake pan and bake until a toothpick inserted in the cake comes out clean, 30 to 35 minutes. Transfer to a rack and let cool completely.

To prepare the peanut butter mousse, in a large bowl, beat cream cheese, peanut butter, and confectioners' sugar with a handheld mixer on medium speed until smooth and fluffy, about 3 minutes. Put cream into a large bowl and beat on high speed until stiff peaks form. Using a rubber spatula, fold the whipped cream into the peanut butter mixture; set mousse aside in the refrigerator.

To assemble the cake, use a serrated-blade knife to slice each cake horizontally into two layers. Place one layer of the devil's food cake on a cake stand and spread one-third of the peanut butter mousse over the top with a butter knife. Top mousse with a layer of the angel food cake and spread with half of the remaining mousse. Repeat with the remaining devil's food cake, mousse, and angel food cake. Wrap cake in plastic wrap and freeze for 2 hours. Stir ganache until smooth and spread evenly over the top and sides of the cake with a butter knife. Refrigerate the cake for 2 hours before slicing. Serves 10 to 12.

abacus | jasper's

AT AN AGE ALMOST AS TENDER AS THE RESULTING BRISKET AND RIBS, Kent Rathbun learned to be the perfect Texas cook. Watching his father, Kent saw the peculiar magic of "low and slow," the application of low temperatures for long periods of time. And he suffered the slings and arrows of 10, 12, or 15 hours of cooking, being deputized by his dad to get up several times a night to baste meat on the family smoker. By the time Kent had reached his teens, he was the ultimate Texas cooking machine.

Except that he was in Kansas City.

His story as a chef, growing up in a place that can lay claim (along with Memphis and the Carolinas) to some of the best barbecue outside the Lone Star State, is one long demonstration of the popular bumper sticker "I Wasn't Born in Texas but I Got Here as Quick as I Could." Along that road, Kent mastered quite a few cuisines that would lead him far beyond his father's backyard mentorship. And then, once his restaurants in Dallas established his reputation nationally, they proved they could lead him home as well.

"I started from the bottom, and I went through the school of hard knocks," offers Kent, and you can tell by the way he says it that it's nothing resembling an apology. "You respect the chefs and the cooks around you, because you know what it takes to peel that gallon of garlic. Sure, we're glad you have that culinary degree when you come looking for a job at Abacus, or at Jasper's, or at Rathbun's Blue Plate Kitchen. But now we have to teach you about *life* in a restaurant."

Kent's career in restaurants may have started at the bottom, resembling the hard-scrabble apprenticeship tradition found in European kitchens more than the "academic" version now dished up by the various culinary institutes. But it has also mirrored his own personal journey to Texas, from home cooking to fancy global cuisine—and back again—right along with the pilgrimage of so many modern American taste buds. By the time America was ready for some serious comfort food, in other words, there were few "gourmet" chefs anywhere quite as ready as Kent Rathbun to give it to them.

Kent grew up in Kansas City as half of what became American cuisine's most famous "brother act," learning the beginnings of cooking alongside his brother Kevin, now a famous chef based in Atlanta. The two brothers soaked up the influence of their father, of course, but also of their mother, who worked over the years at many significant restaurants around the city. According to Kent, this meant the boys grew accustomed to dining out. They knew how to behave in a restaurant, they knew how to order and enjoy different types of food, and they simply gazed at a dining horizon much broader than their friends who mostly ate at home.

And then there were those exchange students from Thailand. They came to live at the Rathbun house for several months, and it being the Rathbun house, that meant they came to cook and eat as well. Before long, Kent remembers, it didn't seem odd to walk in on his father making egg rolls at the kitchen table.

"You respect the chefs and the cooks around you, because you know what it takes to peel that gallon of garlic."

"Kevin knew he wanted to be a chef before me, starting culinary school at 17," recalls Kent. "I was actually 19 or 20 before I started thinking, 'This is something I seem to be good at.' I was lucky enough to get one of my first jobs at a five-star French restaurant, La Bonne Auberge, and that meant working both the front and the back of the house. We cooks had to go out in the dining room and become server's assistants, bussing, setting tables, shining wine glasses. I have to tell you, those experiences sure helped me a lot."

Another part of his long apprenticeship took him to New Orleans, where he was invited to work as sous chef to one of the city's most renowned culinarians, executive chef Gerard Maras. Yet the chef—like the Lord, for a lot of the same reasons—works in mysterious ways. Maras hadn't bothered to mention that Kent would be *competing* with two other guys for that single sous chef job, or that his ability to take it and keep it would depend on his ability to learn. There was a ton to learn from Maras, such as using meats and vegetables from local farmers, a decade before that was *de rigueur*, and butchering your own meats and fish. Today when young chefs come to him without such foundational skills, it's sometimes all Kent can do to not send them packing.

"It's a lost art, butchering," he says. "I can butcher anything you lay in front of me. I've done a lot of it. But today so many restaurants buy pre-cut steaks and pre-cut fish to save money. And the more we do that, the less of a training ground we become for the people who work here."

Kent feels lucky to have made it into high-end dining early, without the typical years in fast-casual cafés and diners. He also considers it a blessing he went to work for a corporate-owned hotel company that, as he puts it, "wanted the sun, the moon, and the stars." This was at the Melrose, the boutique property that brought him to Dallas, where he would eventually make his home. Yet almost as soon as Kent got himself and his stuff settled into this new city, the company winged him off to Thailand to cook Texas food in a two-week promotion. There was something about those sweet, salty, spicy flavors of Thailand, something he remembered from those exchange students. Kent was every bit as ready to learn as he was to teach.

As it turned out, this culinary promotion left the young chef with an eternal travel bug—no, not the kind that makes you ill, but the kind that keeps you traveling. To this day, he leads tours for 50 to 60 of his best customers a couple times a year to places they (or he) want to go. So far the groups have visited several regions of Italy and Spain, as well as California's wine country. And yes, of course, they've been to Thailand.

"I can butcher anything you lay in front of me. I've done a lot of it. But today so many restaurants buy pre-cut steaks and pre-cut fish to save money."

"People pretty much book every trip we do," Kent says without boasting. "But don't kid yourself: I learn as much on these trips as they do. Sure, I'm giving them an experience they could probably never get any other way, but I'm learning everywhere. I have so many things in my head after these trips, there's no way I'm ever going to be able to implement them all."

In 1977, Kent saw an opportunity to do something chefs before and after him have done—parlay the fame of cooking at the Melrose and at the Mansion on Turtle Creek into a restaurant of his own. Located in Dallas's Uptown section, Abacus was born as a tribute to humankind's ability to enjoy eating just about anything, made by some of the most talented cooks with some of the most spectacular ingredients. As you might expect, Asian flavors played a significant role at Abacus, but not to the point that they knocked all other flavors out of balance—doing that, of course, wouldn't be very Asian.

To this day, diners who sit down for dinner are greeted by a lengthy list of sushi, both traditional and innovative rolls, plus (for purists) a wide array of nigiri and sashimi. Such choices fit gracefully into Kent's vision of 4- or even 9-course chef's tasting menus, preferably with a wine chosen for each course. But whether you choose what comes next or let the kitchen choose for you, you are destined for quite a few surprises. Everything on the menu at Abacus, it seems, is about creative uses of ingredients, including splashy applications of the delightfully down-home. There is no chicken fried steak on the menu, for instance, but there is chicken fried Texas bobwhite quail, paired up with Yukon whipped potatoes and red-eye gravy.

In lieu of classic appetizers there are Small Plates, so it only makes sense that in lieu of entrees there would be Big Plates. And in the World of Kent Rathbun, if you call something big it had better show up that way. One of the best bets may well be the hickory-grilled lamb strip loins (that whole butcher thing again) with bleu-cheese corn grits and chipotle oil. Food full of comfort that also happens to be food full of surprises. And in the least expected follow-up to all that sushi, Kent has over the years appended an entire steakhouse concept onto his Abacus menu, under the straightforward title Abacus Prime.

By the time his Abacus had been embraced by Dallas as one of the two or three destinations that put the city on the dining map, Kent was already dreaming about something else. And if a few memories of grilling and smoking meats with his father had found their way onto corners of his first global menu, they'd take their place front-and-center at Jasper's Gourmet Backyard Cuisine. Opening first in suburban Plano and then spinning off

Abacus was born as a tribute to humankind's ability to enjoy eating just about anything.

locations in the Woodlands north of Houston as well as in Austin, Jasper's was the ultimate barbecue joint for people who secretly yearn for an evening of casual fine dining.

Meats are dominant and large at Jasper's, nearly all of them cooked low and slow in the manner of backyards all over Texas. Still, being a chef, Kent is allowed to go even those time-honored techniques one better, as he demonstrates on his slow-smoked baby back ribs with creamy baked potato salad and ancho barbecue. A whole series of different methods is called into play to make each rib combine the intense flavors of smoking with the moist tenderness of braising. You can build out from these amazing ribs with a chopped wedge salad with applewood smoked bacon, crispy onion rings, and bleu cheese at the start and one or more of the chef's dozen "cast iron sides."

Quite naturally, all such thinking about the foods of his childhood pointed Kent inexorably toward what he came to call Rathbun's Blue Plate Kitchen. By this point in his journey, all notions of fancy food were tossed aside, except perhaps the iron-fisted, no-compromise demand for quality. The Kitchen is like a country diner that still tells you where the cheese and cherries come from. With main dishes like the Blue Plate "Meatblock" (even the name sounds good) with roasted onion pan gravy and DP Mopped Rotisserie Chicken (DP meaning Dr Pepper, naturally), it takes no great imagination to imagine that people used to eat like this. Well, they didn't —but they surely wished they did.

"Comfort. Cuisine."

That's what the menu promises at Rathbun's Blue Plate Kitchen. And with allowances for decades of cooking some of the world's most exciting foods for some of the world's most discriminating diners, that's what Kent has been about since he was a five-year-old rising in the night to baste the brisket on his father's pit.

LOBSTER SCALLION SHOOTERS:

2	ounces sesame oil	1	bunch scallions, chopped
4	cloves garlic, minced	2	tablespoons mint, chopped
2	shallots, minced	2	tablespoons basil, chopped
1	stalk lemongrass, minced	32	dumpling wrappers
2	ounces ginger, peeled and minced	2	eggs, whipped
1	pound lobster meat (cooked), chopped fine	1	cup cornstarch
¼	cup tamari soy sauce	3	cups peanut oil
2	tablespoons sambal chili sauce		

In a medium sauté pan, sauté the garlic, shallots, lemongrass, and ginger in sesame oil until slightly browned. Remove from heat and transfer to a mixing bowl. Fold in the lobster meat, soy sauce, sambal, scallions, mint, and basil. Lay out dumpling wrappers evenly on a flat surface, then brush a thin layer of egg on each wrapper. Place a small amount of the mixture in the center of the wrapper. Fold the edges of the wrappers up around the mixture and squeeze the edges to seal the dumpling. Spread the cornstarch on a cookie sheet and lay dumplings on the cornstarch (this helps to keep them dry and crunchy). Deep-fry dumplings in 350-degree peanut oil until golden brown. Serve with red curry–coconut sauce.

THAI RED CURRY–COCONUT SAUCE:

2	ounces sesame oil	½	cup sake
2	tablespoons minced garlic	2	tablespoons red curry paste
4	tablespoons minced shallots	1	quart coconut milk
2	tablespoons peeled and chopped ginger	1	ounce cornstarch, for thickening if necessary
2	tablespoons chopped lemongrass, white part only	2	tablespoons chopped cilantro leaves
2	kaffir lime leaves, chopped	2	tablespoons chopped mint leaves
½	cup rice vinegar, seasoned	2	tablespoons chopped Thai basil leaves
½	cup mirin	2	limes, juiced and zested

In a small sauce pan, add sesame oil and lightly sauté the garlic, shallots, ginger, and lemongrass until translucent (do not brown). Add kaffir lime leaves and cover with rice vinegar, mirin, and sake, and continue cooking until liquid is reduced by half. Stir in red curry paste, add coconut milk, and bring to a boil. Thicken to sauce consistency with cornstarch mixture if needed. Steep cilantro, mint, and Thai basil for 10 minutes. Finish with lime juice and zest. Strain through a fine chinois. Serves 8.

CHIPOTLE–MOLASSES GLAZED BACON:

3	ounces canned chipotles
1	cup molasses
1	ounce whole-grain mustard
3	ounces Heinz ketchup
3	cloves garlic, chopped
1	lime, juiced
1	teaspoon kosher salt
3	pounds Niman Ranch chipotle bacon, cut into 8 ⅜-inch-thick slices

DUCK EGGS:

8	duck eggs, cracked and set aside in a bowl
1	teaspoon kosher salt
1	tablespoon whole butter
½	ounce truffle oil
½	ounce whole black truffle, grated or chopped
2	tablespoons chives, snipped
8	slices brioche bread (our favorite type of bread), toasted

In a blender, combine chipotles, molasses, whole-grain mustard, ketchup, and garlic. Blend together until smooth. Add lime juice and kosher salt. Strain through fine mesh chinois. Grill bacon slices on both sides, until rendered and crispy. Brush bacon with molasses glaze before serving.

In a mixing bowl, whisk duck eggs and kosher salt until smooth. In a sauté pan, add whole butter and truffle oil and set on medium heat. When whole butter is melted, add duck egg mixture and begin to scramble eggs (keep them soft). Garnish with grated black truffle and chives.

On a plate, using a pastry brush, make a brush stroke with the molasses glaze. Place a slice of toasted brioche on the plate. Place a spoonful of scrambled eggs on top of brioche toast.

Place Niman Ranch chipotle bacon on side of the plate, and drizzle chipotle-molasses glaze on top. Serves 8.

SAUCE:

1   tablespoon canola oil
1   tablespoon peeled and chopped garlic
1   tablespoon peeled and chopped shallot
2   cups fresh pineapple juice
1   vanilla bean, split
1   cup heavy cream
1   pound butter, cubed
2   teaspoons kosher salt
1   cup pineapple, diced

In a medium sauce pan, add canola oil and sauté shallots and garlic until translucent. Deglaze with pineapple juice, add vanilla bean, and reduce by half. Add heavy cream, continue cooking, and reduce by half. Slowly whisk in butter a little at a time, making sure that each cube is incorporated before adding the next. Season with salt, and pass through a fine chinois. Add diced pineapple.

SWORDFISH:

8   swordfish steaks, 7 ounces each and 1-inch thick
2   ounces extra-virgin olive oil
2   tablespoons kosher salt

Rub swordfish fillets with olive oil and season with kosher salt. Grill fillets over a wood fire until done. Swordfish should be done but be careful not to overcook and dry them out. Serve swordfish with pineapple-vanilla butter sauce and black rice (see recipe, page 126).

PINEAPPLE CHIPS:

16   pineapple slices, peeled and sliced paper thin

Preheat the oven to 200° F.

Place pineapple slices on a silicone baking sheet and bake for 40 to 45 minutes until crisp. Use chips as a garnish for the swordfish. Serves 8.

COCONUT BLACK RICE

RICE:
1 ounce sesame oil
2 tablespoons minced garlic
2 tablespoons minced shallots
2 tablespoons peeled and minced ginger
2 tablespoons minced lemongrass
2 cups Chinese black rice
¼ cup mirin
1 quart chicken stock
2 cups coconut milk
1 tablespoon stemmed and chopped chiles de arbol
2 limes, juiced and zested
2 tablespoons fish sauce
2 tablespoons soy sauce

GARNISH:
1 ounce sesame oil
4 ounces shiitake mushrooms, thinly sliced
1 red bell pepper, seeds and membrane removed, diced
1 yellow bell pepper, seeds and membrane removed, diced
½ cup diced carrot
½ cup chopped scallions

In a large pot over medium heat, sauté the garlic, shallots, ginger, and lemongrass in sesame oil until translucent. Add black rice and continue stirring slowly. Deglaze with mirin and add a cup of the chicken stock. When rice kernels absorb the liquid, add another cup of the chicken stock and continue cooking, repeating this process until all the chicken stock is used. Add the coconut milk and continue cooking until rice is creamy. Season with chile de arbol, lime juice and zest, fish sauce, and soy sauce.

In a wok or large sauté pan, sauté the mushrooms, red and yellow peppers, carrots, and scallions in sesame oil until tender. Stir into the rice and serve. Serves 8.

SAUCE:

- 8 ounces smoked bacon, diced (one ham hock may be substituted)
- 1 cup onion (smoked or grilled), coarsely chopped
- 4 cloves garlic (smoked or grilled), chopped
- 2 chiles de arbol, stem removed
- 2 cups peaches (fresh or dried), coarsely chopped
- 1 tablespoon cracked black pepper
- 2 tablespoons Worcestershire sauce
- 2 cups fresh orange juice
- 2 cups ketchup
- 6 dashes Tabasco sauce
- 2 tablespoons fresh lemon juice
- 2 teaspoons kosher salt

PORK:

- 8 pieces pork tenderloin (about 8 ounces each), trimmed of fat and silver skin
- 3 ounces olive oil
- 2 tablespoons cracked black pepper
- 2 tablespoons kosher salt
- 1 tablespoon granulated garlic

In a small sauce pan, cook bacon on medium heat until crisp, then add onions and garlic and sauté until caramelized. Add chiles de arbol and continue to cook until chiles start to toast. Add peaches and black pepper, and deglaze with Worcestershire sauce and orange juice. Reduce orange juice until it starts to thicken. Add ketchup and reduce to low heat. Continue cooking for about 15 minutes. Season with Tabasco sauce, lemon juice, and salt. Strain barbecue sauce and set aside.

On a sheet pan, rub tenderloins with olive oil and season with cracked black pepper, kosher salt, and granulated garlic. Grill over an open flame or on a charbroiler until desired temperature is reached. (Medium rare is best.) Serve sliced with the peach barbecue sauce. Garnish with crispy fried onions. Serves 8.

1   *French baguette (18 inches), sliced ½-inch thick*
8   *ounces white chocolate, chopped*
8   *ounces dried cherries*
1   *cup sugar*
1   *tablespoon cinnamon*
1   *teaspoon nutmeg*
6   *large eggs*
2   *cups heavy cream*
2   *cups milk*
1   *tablespoon vanilla extract*
4   *ounces butter*
4   *ounces cherry jelly*

Preheat the oven to 325° F.

Place sliced bread in a large mixing bowl. Add white chocolate and dried cherries. In a separate mixing bowl combine sugar, cinnamon, and nutmeg. Set aside about ¼ cup of this mixture for later. Add the eggs, cream, milk, and vanilla to the sugar mixture and mix thoroughly. Pour custard over the bread and mix, making sure all of the bread is soaked. Transfer to a large baking pan. Evenly place the butter slices on top and sprinkle remaining sugar mixture over the top of the bread pudding. Bake until golden brown and center is set, about 50 to 60 minutes. Remove from the oven, spread cherry jelly evenly on top, and serve. This recipe works great as single portions also. Serves 8.

bonnell's

▼▼▼▼▼▼▼▼▼▼▼▼▼▼▼

"COOKING IS WHAT HAPPENS," OFFERS EXECUTIVE CHEF JON BONNELL, "when chemistry, physics, and math work together on biology."

And he should know.

Before he went to culinary school, became a chef, and opened his own restaurant in Fort Worth—that act alone requiring courage in the traumatic days after September 11, 2001—Jon was a high school science teacher. And while his attire has definitely changed, he still carries to each table in Bonnell's Fine Texas Cuisine the aw-shucks charm that probably worked on his students, the kind that doesn't sound like he's merely showing them a discovery but *discovering* it right along with them. If he wanted to, if he weren't so busy at the restaurant between lunch and dinner each day, Jon could probably slip over to the nearest high school and knock out a period or two of freshman biology. And he'd have to change nothing except his suit.

As Texas chefs go, Jon is intellectually serious and wildly curious about why and how food does what it does; but for several reasons, he wears his scholarly side lightly. For one thing, he was born and brought up in Fort Worth, that proudly self-proclaimed "cowtown" despite its plethora of world-class museums and performing arts venues. In Fort Worth, the cooking of the Texas countryside is neither forgotten nor far away, with foods like beef, beef, and more beef, plus chicken fried steak, barbecue, chili, and other down-home flavors on even the most refined diner's list of favorites.

Fort Worth spends an inordinate amount of time *not* being like New York, Los Angeles, or Chicago. And it spends the most time of all not being like Dallas. To fall more than a little in thrall to Asian flavors or to Peruvian sushi or to so-called molecular gastronomy would, in the eyes of Jon and his talented local peers, reek of being a chef over in Dallas. Not an acceptable outcome at all.

"My mother was good at making classic recipes by the book, you know, lots of things that were American or maybe even French," recalls Jon, the fourth generation of his family to call Fort Worth home. "She threw a lot of dinner parties. My dad was more of a seat-of-your-pants kind of Texas cook, always hunting and fishing. 'Let's do big stuff' seemed to be his culinary motto. He was the first guy around, for instance, who had to try beer-can chicken on the backyard grill. I learned a lot from both of them but especially my appetite for the outdoors and for all meats. I still have this great image of spending time in the outdoors with my dad."

Though Jon was inducted into the "Texas guy" cooking culture by his father, it was still several years before he was able to combine both his parents' styles and interests into a desire to cook for a living. He picked up a degree in education from Vanderbilt, following his nose to applied sciences and math and finally teaching a wide variety of such subjects in Fort Worth middle and high schools. After several years in the classroom, though, Jon decided something was missing. It wasn't a lack of daily challenge, as any teacher will assure you, nor even the

"My mother was good at making classic recipes by the book, you know, lots of things that were American or maybe even French," recalls Jon.

lack of huge earning potential. To hear him tell the tale now, teaching let him concentrate on a single thing *too long* at one time.

"In a restaurant, especially if you own the place, you have to keep your ear out for five different things at once," Jon laughs, deftly sidestepping the current alphabet soup of conditions that always includes the letters ADD. "That really works well for my brain. To me, being here is like being the conductor of a symphony orchestra."

Still, to become the conductor he envisioned, Jon figured he'd better learn something about music. Or, in his case, the technical side of cooking, mixed with the business side of running a restaurant. After shopping around, he ended up pursuing his studies at the New England Culinary Institute in Montpelier, Vermont, and then making his way to and through a life-changing "externship" at Mr. B's Bistro in the French Quarter of New Orleans.

As it has for many chefs from all over America, and in some cases the world, New Orleans proved an eye-opener for Jon. Still, it wasn't only the spicy, savory, intensely layered flavors of Creole and Cajun that intrigued him and inflamed him for his new career; it was also the legendary Brennan family, who had years earlier at Commander's Palace in the Garden District mastered the art of serving lots of diners extremely good food. Among trained chefs, it's tacitly understood that almost anyone can knock the socks off people if your dining room seats ten or twenty. But to remove those socks day after day, night after night, for, at times, more than a thousand people at a time—that takes talent, that takes systems, and that takes a calm, cold-eyed version of genius. Jon was hooked—no, not on phonics but on high-volume fine dining.

"The cooking is the easiest part," Jon says of the job he created for himself by opening Bonnell's. "The hardest part in the restaurant business is managing your personnel." He stops a moment, perhaps to assign himself a letter grade. But then he remembers the only grade that matters when it comes to employees. "Most of our kitchen staff has been here since the day we opened. I feel like we've got a well-oiled machine." He grins, maybe a tiny bit wickedly. "But I'm still here every day."

For his first restaurant, Jon settled on a cooking style—somewhere along the way he started calling it "Fine Texas Cuisine," with an echo of the Brennan family's "haute Creole"—that weds the native Texan's lifelong love affair with beef and all forms of game to a fascination with fresh seafood from the Texas Gulf Coast. In the beginning of his menu writing, there were numerous *homages* to New Orleans, of which his still wildly popular Oysters Texasfeller is a legacy. Over the months of creating, however, and especially over the years of serving Fort Worth customers, Jon has found his way to the flavors that make them keep coming back.

"You cannot impose your will," he says realistically, not seeming to know how many of his chef brethren *haven't* figured this part out yet. "People want to eat what they want. I grew up here in Texas, with all those wonderful Tex-Mex flavors. Without anybody telling me, I *knew* how to make guacamole. That's just in your blood when you're a Texan."

So, it seems, was that Texas entrepreneurial spirit. Thinking through the guest experience backward and forward, Jon formed his vision of Bonnell's in the months leading up to its opening in the fall of 2001. Including what he loved and excluding what he hated about other fine-dining establishments—the Brennans, no doubt, had helped him develop this skill—Jon roughed out an eatery of extreme comfort and wonderful Texas-themed food.

He'd learned to love wines, so he made them a major part of his menu and his business plan. And since he hated the feeling of a large dining room with diners stranded way out in the middle, he used partial walls to create a series of intimate nooks within his 150-seat space so every table, as he likes to boast, can be a corner table. Not surprisingly, considering all Jon believes about food, wine, and service, the feeling is less of a busy restaurant than of a comfortable Texas home. As though to make the connection obvious, Jon covered the walls with his own color photographs of wildlife and bits of rustic scenery from the Bonnell family ranch.

As opening day approached, hopes were high at Bonnell's Fine Texas Cuisine. The place might even open sometime that September, if the final construction and decoration pieces came together. But then 9/11 happened. After the initial shock waves of the tragedy settled over America, what remained was a nation so committed to staying home—for months, maybe for years?—that even established restaurants struggled. Surely opening a new restaurant would be foolish in the months after the terrorist attacks on the World Trade Center and the Pentagon.

"The cooking is the easiest part. The hardest part in the restaurant business is managing your personnel." Jon says.

But Jon Bonnell wasn't born a Texan for nothing. Bonnell's opened on October 12. If you look hard at the large tile mosaic behind the hostess stand, you will pick out an American flag woven into the design in the frightening days after 9/11. It is Jon's reminder of his venture's opening, and of all the freedoms he treasures as a Texan and as an American.

All these years of success later, Jon still walks the same fine line he has since Day One, between expressing his food curiosity and giving customers what they want to order every single visit. "If I stop serving the green chile-cheese grits," he chuckles, "there's going to be a revolution." For sheer creativity, there are the five-course wine dinners he offers regularly, with no holds barred except a broad understanding of his customers' tastes. And there's the cooking classes he teaches, many times more classes than the typical "celeb-chef," at Fort Worth's Central Market and far beyond. Having come up with more than 300 dishes since opening the doors to Bonnell's, only a fraction of which can fit on any reasonable menu, he has to aim these things somewhere.

All these years of success later, Jon still walks the same fine line he has since Day One, between expressing his food curiosity and giving customers what they want to order every single visit.

Jon also balances his life by spending time with his wife, Melinda (from Graham, Texas), and his two-year-old daughter, Charlotte, who "already loves to cook and eats everything. She had fried oysters yesterday." The chef sees one or more cookbooks in his future, perhaps expanding from his first published effort to one celebrating Gulf Coast seafood. Maybe, he says, there's another fine-dining restaurant in him, but probably no more than that. And in hyper-organized teacher fashion, he wants the menu there to showcase the recipes developed for his seafood cookbook. More cooking classes, of course. And perhaps television, whenever that opportunity knocks.

"Cooking at home," Jon observes, with more than a little understanding, "starts with a series of recipes you know you're comfortable with. But professional cooking starts when you learn proper techniques. Then you can cook anything, not just one thing. Once you know sauté in your sleep, you can sauté anything. Then you can get creative and start playing bigger games." The chef smiles, as though caught reverting to his previous life. "You see, I still love to teach."

OYSTERS TEXASFELLER

OYSTERS:

1   dozen Galveston Bay oysters
⅔   cup buttermilk
1   tablespoon Crystal hot sauce
1   cup all-purpose flour
2   tablespoons Creole seasoning
1   shallot, minced
1   clove garlic, minced

1   teaspoon butter
3   ounces tasso ham, diced
2   cups chopped fresh spinach
1   bunch cilantro, chopped
½   ounce dry white wine
¼   teaspoon kosher salt

Clean and shuck the Texas oysters and remove from shells. Discard only the top halves of the oyster shells. Marinate the oysters in a mixture of the buttermilk and hot sauce for at least 2 hours. This can be done overnight, but must be kept cold. Dredge the oysters in a mixture of the flour and Creole seasoning until well coated. Fry the oysters in 375-degree oil for approximately 1 to 2 minutes. Drain on a paper towel.

Over medium heat, sweat the shallots and garlic in butter in a sauté pan. Add the diced tasso, then top with spinach and cilantro. Splash in a bit of dry white wine and cook just until the spinach is wilted. To be safe, the oyster shells can be boiled before using. Fill each shell with the spinach mixture, then place one oyster on top of each and spoon a silky layer of hollandaise sauce on top.

HOLLANDAISE SAUCE:

3   egg yolks
1½ tablespoons dry white wine
1   teaspoon hot sauce
1½ teaspoons lemon juice

1   pinch ground red pepper
½   teaspoon salt
1   cup clarified butter

Slowly cook egg yolks, wine, and hot sauce over a double boiler while whisking. When the yolks have doubled in volume, add remaining ingredients except for the butter. Slowly drizzle the butter in while whisking vigorously. Season with salt to taste. Store in a warm place until ready to use. Do not refrigerate or reheat. This is a very unstable sauce that must be served immediately. Serves 4 to 6.

ROASTED TOMATO AND JALAPEÑO SOUP

3 to 4 fresh jalapeños
15 ripe Roma tomatoes
1   extra-large sweet onion, sliced into large rings
3 to 4 cloves garlic, chopped

Extra-virgin olive oil
Juice of 2 limes
1 ¼ teaspoon kosher salt
½   teaspoon Creole seasoning blend

Slice the jalapeños in half, cut off the stems, and remove half of the white veins and seeds. Grill the tomatoes, jalapeños, and onion until well charred on the outsides. In a large soup pot, lightly simmer the onions, tomatoes, jalapeños, and garlic with a touch of olive oil and 1 ½ cups of water for 1 to 2 hours. Puree with a stick blender and strain. Add lime juice and season with salt and Creole seasoning. Serves 4 to 6.

Optional: Garnish the top with a little lime-flavored sour cream and chopped cilantro or jalapeño slices.

PECAN-CRUSTED TEXAS REDFISH WITH BABY SHRIMP,

TOMATO, AND CILANTRO BUTTER SAUCE

2 ounces Creole seasoning
½ cup fresh pecan halves
1 (8-ounce) fillet of fresh redfish, boneless and
   skinless (grouper or red snapper is also excellent)
5 to 7 baby shrimp
1 small shallot, minced
½ clove garlic, minced
2 to 3 ounces dry white wine
1 ounce chopped tomato
1 teaspoon chopped cilantro
3 tablespoons butter
1 tablespoon olive oil
Salt and pepper
½ lime, juiced

Mix the Creole seasoning with pecan halves and pulse in a food processor several times until the nuts only have a few large pieces left, then scatter the mix out on a large plate. Lay the clean and dry fish fillet down on top of the seasonings and press lightly to get the nuts to stick. Be sure to lay the pretty side (or what we in the industry call the presentation side) down in the nuts. They will end up facing up on the finished plate.

In a medium-hot pan, drizzle a little olive oil in, then gently place the fish fillet inside, pecan side down. Gently shake the pan back and forth just a little to keep the fish from sticking to the bottom of the pan. Nonstick pans work exceptionally well for cooking fish. Cook on the first side for approximately 1 ½ to 2 minutes, being careful not to let the nuts burn. If the pecans turn black and smoke, the dish must be started over using a cooler pan. Turn the fillet over gently and continue cooking until the fish is done. If the fish is very thick, place the entire pan into a 375-degree oven (as long as it's an oven-safe pan) and finish cooking in the oven after flipping.

Remove fillet from the pan and let rest on a warm plate while you make the sauce. Add shrimp, shallots, and garlic to the same fish pan; turn up the heat to high and sauté lightly. Add the white wine and allow it to reduce by a little more than half. Add the tomatoes, cilantro, and butter. Swirl the entire contents continually until the butter melts. Season lightly with salt and pepper, squeeze in the lime juice, and pour over the fish fillet and serve immediately. Serves 1.

GOAT CHEESE AND PINE NUT—CRUSTED BEEF TENDERLOIN

2	tablespoons pinenuts	1	(7-ounce) beef tenderloin fillet
1	teaspoon chopped thyme	2	pinches kosher salt
1	teaspoon chopped chives	1	pinch freshly ground black pepper
½	clove garlic, minced	½	teaspoon canola oil
2	ounces fresh Texas goat cheese		

Lightly toast the pinenuts in a dry nonstick pan to a light golden brown. Combine the herbs, garlic, and goat cheese, and mix with a pinch of salt. Season the fillet with salt and pepper, then sear in canola oil. Be sure to brown each side of the fillet before turning over to really caramelize the outside. If the beef is thick, it may be necessary to finish cooking in the oven. Cook to desired temperature. When the beef is almost finished, smother the top with the herb goat cheese mixture and place in the oven for 1 minute to warm the cheese. Top with the toasted pinenuts and serve. Serves 1.

Dr Pepper Float:

2   scoops premium vanilla ice cream
1   bottle Dublin Original Dr Pepper
Whipped cream
Cinnamon buñuelo cookies (see recipe)

In a frosted glass (put into freezer ahead of time), place two scoops of ice cream, then slowly pour in the Dr Pepper. Top with whipped cream then strips of cinnamon cookies, and serve.

Cinnamon Buñuelo Cookies:

2   *flour tortillas*
2   *tablespoons sugar*
1 ½ *teaspoons ground cinnamon*
Vegetable oil

Cut the tortillas into any shape desired. At the restaurant, we make them into stars and the shape of Texas with cookie cutters. We also cut into thin strips for garnish. Combine the sugar and cinnamon together and mix. Fry the tortillas in 350-degree vegetable oil until crispy, then sprinkle with cinnamon sugar until well coated. This needs to be done while the tortillas are still hot and fresh from the oil. Serves 1.

Note: The original formula for Dr Pepper is available only from the folks in Dublin, Texas. It's far superior to the regular brand and true Texans travel from miles around just to stock up on the original.

uchi | uchiko

uchi | uchiko

FLORIDA-BORN, TEXAS-SCULPTED TYSON COLE has a lovely wife and two beautiful daughters. But when he pulls out his iPhone to show a visitor a photograph, it isn't of a wobbly first step or a festive third birthday. The photo shows a raw slab of Kobe-style short ribs on a cutting board, the first step to the grilled beef, heirloom peaches, apple, and tiny okra now gracing the table. Having painfully worked his way inside the Japanese mind by way of the cuisine and even the language, he knows you can't understand anything without understanding where it came from.

"I take pictures of everything," says Tyson, who opened Uchi with business partner Daryl Kunik in 2003 and quickly found his own smiling face on the cover of *Food and Wine* magazine. "I download all these photos to my computer at home about once a month. It's a kind of diary, if you will."

While still under 40, Tyson has plenty to put in anybody's idea of a diary. He has spent close to 15 years doing what must have once seemed impossible, overcoming not only his own ignorance of Japanese ways but also the prejudice of many Japanese chefs toward anybody who isn't one of them. Early resentment grew into Texas-sized anger, which in turn grew into steely determination to succeed. Uchi undeniably qualifies as a success, with the original 100-seat location packed every night of the week and a second location called Uchiko opening to much fanfare in 2010.

"This is a *very* Austin restaurant," he offers. "You can spend $20 or $2,000. You can come in a suit or in shorts and sandals."

Indeed, what has emerged from Tyson's kitchen—and even more profoundly from Tyson's soul—is something authentically Japanese, born of a culture, a history, and a set of spiritual concepts that direct all things a pair of hands can do with food. Yet at the same time, what has emerged is profoundly American; you might say it's something no Japanese master could have done. Tyson has reimagined all that's meaningful about Japanese cuisine with a dizzying respect for tradition, yet also with that American genius for starting down a brand new road each day. From the moment his restaurant welcomed its first customers into a wonderland of red floral wallpaper and Tiffany blue ceilings, savvy Austinites knew they were experiencing something never exactly seen before. Anywhere.

"What we call 'Uchi food' is quality ingredients, done simply, put together the right way," the chef explains, setting down a definition that isn't as simple to execute as it is to express. "Everything here is clean, light, and crisp. It's the way people eat these days." Tyson glances around the dining room, where the rumble of conversation is fast approaching a roar as the summer sun slips down. He picks something out of this swirling tapestry and laughs, almost to himself: "If you wanna have a successful restaurant these days, you better make damn sure women like your food. They're the ones who decide *everything*."

"This is a very Austin restaurant. You can spend $20 or $2,000. You can come in a suit or in shorts and sandals."

In Japanese, "Uchi" means house, or even more compellingly, home. That speaks to the heart of the restaurant's warmth and welcome in (or perhaps despite) a cuisine often associated in this country with being cold, serious, almost surgical. Uchi is both what Tyson wants it to be and has the food he wants it to serve, mixed with a generous helping of what the space actually was. Uchi used to *be* a home, and while the vision of space designer Michael Hsu joins forces with furniture, fabrics, and finishes by Joel Mozersky, both went the extra mile to preserve the residential feel. Few Americans will ever experience dinner in a home in Japan. Uchi is what we wish it would be.

Seriousness and irreverence are precariously balanced within Tyson Cole. Despite the mind-bending devotion to Japanese food his long journey has required, Tyson is still more likely to discuss Uchi in terms of atmosphere and feelings, in terms of service style, in terms of fun. A visitor reading only reviews of Uchi's food will invariably be surprised by how un-somber its creator is in person. And that, as with the digital photo of those raw short ribs, has everything to do with where he came from.

No fancy culinary degrees adorn his walls or pad his printed resume. Indeed, for much of his younger life, Tyson didn't realize he wanted to be a chef at all. Between the ages of 12 and 22, it seemed he was trying to put the "odd" back into odd jobs. He worked as a baseball umpire and a kayak instructor, among the more notable of 40 or so outings. A latchkey child of a military family in Sarasota, Tyson remembers nothing in particular about the food he ate growing up. He claims he may be the victim of "aluminum poisoning," from downing too many TV dinners.

This is the culinary training of many a restaurant dishwasher, so appropriately he became one, with no aspirations in the industry beyond that. But the restaurant he washed dishes in was Japanese, and it specialized in sushi; that opened a door for Tyson that no amount of force has ever managed to close. "It looked like they were playing," he recalls. He also recalls that these sushi chefs excited the latent artist deep within him, as though they were making paintings on white canvas with the shapes and colors of fish. Tyson the dishwasher begged the sushi chefs to teach him, but all they did was laugh in his face and tell him to get back to his dishes.

Still, if there's one universal truth, it's that the job you want will open up without notice, probably on the busiest night of the year, if you stick around a little while. One night at that first Austin restaurant, called Kyoto, the sushi chefs found themselves seriously shorthanded, and they asked the young American to pitch in. The dishwasher learned fast and well, eventually becoming Kyoto's head sushi chef and soon after that moving on to Austin's Musashino, where he worked under the sushi chef who became his *sensei* (mentor), Takehiko Fuse.

Few Americans will ever experience dinner in a home in Japan. Uchi is what we wish it would be.

It was during nearly seven years beside Fuse that Tyson visited Japan and learned a lifetime's worth of Japanese culture and language. He had no choice: It was the vocabulary of his trade. He also, though, interacted with lots of American customers at his sushi bar. Tyson didn't quite realize it at the time, but that's when he learned what Americans like and don't like about sushi. And that's when, night after long night, the idea of Uchi was born.

"You develop confidence in whatever your trade is over time," Tyson explains without pretense, thinking back to those days, "while you're getting responses to what you're creating. You develop a repertoire of things you're making that are hits, and of course some things that are misses. Eventually, if you stay with it, you have quite a bit to work off of."

Today, assisted by chef de cuisine Paul Qui ("It took me four years and four other chefs to find the right guy," Tyson says), two sous chefs, and an experienced pastry chef, the American once rejected by Japanese chefs has become an internationally recognized master of their cuisine. On any given night, dinner at Uchi might be chosen from the "permanent" menu, described as "tastings" and divided into "cool" and "hot," or it might come from an equally lengthy list of nightly specials. Or it might encompass a full chef's tasting menu, offered in six or eleven courses, with a wild array of wines and cold sakes for pairing.

The permanent tastings at first seem more traditional than the specials, but even they (carefully considered) draw repeatedly on unexpected Western approaches to fat as well as seasoning. The popular machi cure, for instance, brings on maplewood-smoked baby yellowtail with yucca chips, Asian pear, marcona almonds, and garlic brittle. And the hot list turns up tempura-fried brie with green-tea salt, fresh apple, and crispy sweet potato. Because this early evening in Austin is a particularly steamy one, from the nightly specials comes a fresh, cooling plate of Maine lobster with sweet melon, kaffir lime, and Japanese cucumber in a sparkling lemongrass-coconut vinaigrette. Who can say precisely what culture such creations come from? Under their spell, really, who can care?

"When people go out to eat these days, they have a really short attention span and want to experience as much as possible," Tyson says, speaking clearly of a generation now nourished by Twitter and Facebook as much as by food. "Translation: they want to experience a bunch of different stuff. That whole appetizer-entree-dessert thing is over. And it's boring."

Boredom seems unlikely around Uchi in 2010, with the new location opening in Austin's fast-developing Uptown section. The original Uchi, Tyson points out, is on S. Lamar, while the new one is on N. Lamar; he likes that. It makes him feel better, it seems, about "working like ten times as hard." Candidly, the two- and even three-hour waits for a table at the original had become an issue with some customers, while the number of staff needing career advancement had grown unwieldy, too. It was time to open a second shop.

As a kind of bribe to himself for all the extra effort, not to mention the additional time he'll be away from wife, Rebekkah, and daughters, Aubrie and Larkin, Tyson is giving the new place a vastly expanded bar area and a private dining room, both guaranteed profit centers. And he's even opened up to a notion once unthinkable and mildly heretical—building an Uchi in the "anti-Austin" known as Houston. He'd insist on getting the second Austin location up and running first, of course.

"It has to have a certain level of class," Tyson says of all versions—past, present, and future. "It's not really any different from architecture or fashion or anything else—you have to respect the materials. I was taught to respect the materials. As chefs, we get caught up sometimes in how artistic and, you know, brilliant we are. But we have a responsibility and that's to the customers. They're the ones who actually eat this food. They're the ones who let us have this job."

"When people go out to eat these days, they have a really short attention span and want to experience as much as possible," Tyson says.

COCONUT MILK SORBET WITH CORN SHJIRU AND TAPIOCA PEARLS

CORN SHJIRU:

6	cups fresh corn kernels
1	quart whole milk
2	cups corn milk, reduced to 1 cup
3	ounces coconut milk
2	tablespoons sugar
1	teaspoon salt

To make corn milk, combine fresh corn kernels (if you cannot get fresh corn kernels, sub with IQF frozen, but never use canned) and milk in a blender. Blend well to combine, pulverizing until a milk forms. Put mixture in a sauce pan over medium-high heat, stirring constantly. The natural starch in the corn will start to thicken the mixture. When mixture reaches the boiling point, reduce heat and continue to whisk until reduced to 1 ¼ cups. Strain cooked mixture through a fine-mesh sieve.

Combine one cup of reduced corn milk (reserving 4 teaspoons for the corn crisp), coconut milk, sugar, and salt. Mix well and cook on stove until sugar has dissolved. Cool over ice bath and reserve, chilled.

COCONUT MILK SORBET:

2	cans coconut milk
¾	cup sugar
¼	cup corn syrup
1	teaspoon salt

In a sauce pan, combine all ingredients and heat until right before the boiling point. Remove from heat, mix well, and cool over ice bath. When mixture is ice cold, freeze in an ice cream maker, according to manufacturer's instructions.

TAPIOCA:

6	cups water
7	ounces small tapioca pearls

Bring 4 cups of water to a boil. Add tapioca to boiling water and let return to a boil, cooking for 3 minutes at boil. Add 2 cups of ice water to pot; let come to a boil. When the pot with tapioca has returned to a boil, strain out the

water, add more cold water, and return to the boiling point. Let this cook for 3 minutes. Repeat the boil, strain, and add cold water method four times. On the last repetition turn off heat at the boiling point and let steep for 25 minutes. Strain out water and add more cold water, bring to a boil, and let gently simmer until pearls are mostly clear. Strain and reserve in warm simple syrup.

CORN CRISP:
1¼ ounces melted butter
¼   cup sugar
4   teaspoons reserved corn milk
1   tablespoon all-purpose flour
Basil and kaffir lime leaves to garnish

In food processor, combine all ingredients and mix very well. Transfer mixture into a container and refrigerate. When ready to bake tuiles, remove batter and let it come to room temperature.

Preheat the oven to 350° F.

Using a ½-ounce scoop, place scoops of batter 2 inches apart on a silicone baking mat. Spread thinly and bake for 7 to 9 minutes. Let cool and remove with a thin metal spatula.

Place a large spoonful of cooked tapioca pearls into a chilled, high-rim bowl. Place a scoop of coconut sorbet on top of tapioca pearls. Place corn crisp across the top of the sorbet and add a chiffonade of basil and kaffir lime leaf to garnish. Pour about 3 ounces of chilled corn shjiru into the bowl. Eat immediately. Serves 4.

POACHED LOBSTER WITH CASHEW CURRY, COCONUT MILK, AND FRESH BASIL

POACHED LOBSTER:
2   *quarts water, plus extra for ice bath*
3   *tablespoons salt*
2   *(1-pound) live lobsters*

To prepare the ice bath, put ice into a large container and add water; it should be about as much water as ice. Reserve bath for shocking lobsters when finished cooking. In a large sauce pan, bring water and salt to a rolling boil. To poach lobsters, drop live lobsters into boiling water. Let lobsters cook for exactly 9 minutes. Remove cooked lobster and immediately put into ice bath to shock and stop the cooking process. Reserve chilled, very cold.

COCONUT CLOUD:
1   *can coconut milk*
½   *teaspoon salt*
Pinch of freshly ground black pepper

Combine coconut milk, salt, and pepper. Chill mixture and whisk very well until fat begins to thicken, similar to a whipped cream. The fatty "whipped" part is the coconut cloud. Reserve this part, chilled.

CASHEW CURRY BUTTER:
1   *tablespoon yellow curry paste*
1   *tablespoon vegetable oil, plus extra*
6   *ounces chopped cashews*
1   *ounce water*

Sweat curry paste in a small sauce pan with 1 tablespoon vegetable oil until it becomes aromatic. Add chopped cashews and continue to cook until cashews are very aromatic and start to brown. Stir while cooking to ensure even cooking. Once cashews have browned and paste is very aromatic, deglaze with water. Cook for another 2 minutes and transfer to a blender. Blend and pour in about 2 tablespoons of oil and blend to reach a crunchy, peanut-butter-like consistency. Reserve at room temperature.

KAFFIR LIME OIL:
1   *shallot*
3   *cloves garlic*
1   *cup vegetable oil*
4   *kaffir lime leaves*

Slice shallots about $1/16$-inch thick on the cross section. Brunoise cloves of garlic and combine with shallot in 1 cup of vegetable oil. Add kaffir lime leaves and gently heat over low heat. Once the oil is fragrant, remove from heat and let steep to develop more flavor. Remove kaffir lime leaves and reserve at room temperature.

POTATO CRISPS:
1   *potato, peeled*
2   *cups vegetable oil*
Salt

Slice potatoes paper thin with a mandoline. Place sliced potato pieces into ice water. In a shallow pan, heat vegetable oil to 325° F. Fry potatoes in oil until crispy and evenly browned. Remove from oil and place on paper towel to drain excess oil. Sprinkle salt on warm fried potato and reserve.

On a rectangular plate, place one large dollop of cashew butter. With the end of a spoon, drag butter across plate in a fluid motion. Slice cleaned lobster meat into four 1-ounce slices. Place lobster and kaffir lime oil in a chilled stainless bowl, making sure to get plenty of the chopped garlic and shallot. Season to taste with salt and black pepper. Toss the meat to coat and lay it across the cashew butter in about ½-inch intervals. Spoon remaining seasoned oil over the top of the plated meat. In between the lobster, place little spoonfuls of coconut cream to form a cloud-like appearance. Finish plate with torn basil leaves and garnish with potato crisps. Serves 4.

SUZUKI TATAKI WITH CLEMENTINE ORANGE AND CORIANDER

CLEMENTINE OIL:
Zest of 2 clementine oranges, fruit reserved
¼   *cup vegetable oil*

Place zest into oil and let steep for as long as possible. We are not removing the zest so it is not as important to let flavor develop for too long.

CLEMENTINE CONFIT:
2   *whole clementine oranges, peeled*
2   *tablespoons sugar*
1   *tablespoon kosher salt*
¼   *cup water*

Peel and segment clementine oranges. Combine remaining ingredients in a sauce pan, and quickly bring to a boil. Cool down and reserve. Place segmented clementine oranges into cooled liquid, squeeze juice from the orange segments, remove the orange segments, and chill the liquid.

CORIANDER SALT:
1   *tablespoon coriander*
¼   *cup kosher salt*

In a spice grinder, finely grind coriander and remove from grinder. Mix kosher salt and ground coriander together. Reserve at room temperature.

SAN BAI ZU:
¼   *cup water*
1½   *teaspoons sugar*
⅛   *teaspoon hon dashi*
1½   *teaspoons soy sauce*
¼   *cup rice wine vinegar*

Heat water and sugar to just below boiling point and remove from heat. Add hon dashi and mix well to dissolve. Add soy sauce and rice wine vinegar. Mix well and refrigerate for later use.

SUZUKI TATAKI:
2   *striped bass fillets, skin on*
Vegetable oil
Kosher salt to taste

Lightly rub skin side of bass with vegetable oil. Season lightly with kosher salt, and cook just the skin side with a propane torch. You are not trying to cook the fish; you just want to crisp the skin. If you do not have a propane torch, you can get the same effect by quickly searing the skin side of the fish in a very hot sauté pan. Once skin is cooked, delicately slice through it, leaving the fillet intact.

Place suzuki slices on rectangular plate with skin side up. Place some of the clementine orange confit randomly on top of fish and over plate, about six slices per plate. Drizzle some of the orange liquid on plate as well. Drip some of the san bai zu throughout the plate and around fish. Next place several small drops of the orange oil, placing them on top of other liquids to get a beaded effect. Sprinkle the plate with some coriander salt and a bit of rice cracker. Finish with a bit of micro fennel. Serve immediately. Serves 4.

TUNA AND GOAT CHEESE SASHIMI

1   large Fuji apple, skin on
3   ounces bigeye tuna
1 ½ tablespoons san bai zu (see recipe)
1   clove garlic, finely diced
Kosher salt and freshly cracked black pepper to taste
1 ½ ounces soft goat cheese
2   teaspoons pumpkin seed oil
1   ounce red shiso microgreens

Slice Fuji apple into about eight thin wedges. Slice tuna into small, bite-size pieces and mix with apple in a chilled stainless bowl with cold san bai zu, garlic, and salt and pepper. Plate seasoned and dressed tuna and apples on chilled plate or bowl, and sprinkle with goat cheese. Add pumpkin oil to plate and garnish with shiso. Finish with another pinch of kosher salt to taste.

SAN BAI ZU:
¼ teaspoon hon dashi powder
1   teaspoon sugar
¼ cup hot water
¼ cup rice wine vinegar
1 ½ teaspoons soy sauce
Pinch of salt

Add hon dashi powder and sugar to hot water, and mix to dissolve. Combine remaining ingredients and chill until use. Serves 4.

Chef's Note: For ultimate results, make sure everything you use is chilled: the mixing bowl, serving bowl, san bai zu, goat cheese, and the tuna. You can substitute bigeye tuna for any sashimi-grade tuna. The apple to tuna ratio should always be even.

WAGYU SHORT RIB WITH PICKLED PEACH, GRILLED ONIONS, AND BEER CURD

JUNIPER GASTRIQUE:

1   cup water
½   cup sugar
½   cup sherry vinegar
2   tablespoons whole juniper berries
2   teaspoons salt

Bring all ingredients to a boil, and continue to cook down until mixture has reached a thick, syrup-like consistency. The bubbles on top of the pot should be large and slow.

FLASH-PICKLED PEACHES:

1   large Texas peach
¾   cup water
½   cup sugar
¼   cup white wine vinegar
1   clove garlic
1   teaspoon black peppercorns
1   teaspoon kosher salt
1   cinnamon stick

Wash and slice peaches off the pit into eight ½-inch thick slices. Combine all ingredients, except for peaches, in a medium-size sauce pan and bring to a boil. In a separate stainless bowl, place sliced peaches and pour boiling pickling liquid over the fruit to achieve a flash-pickling effect. Cool down and reserve in liquid.

BEER CURD:

3   egg yolks
2   tablespoons sugar
12 ounces beer
4   ounces butter, cubed, room temperature
1   teaspoon salt

Combine egg yolks, sugar, and beer in a large stainless steel bowl, and mix well. Bring a pot of water to a boil, and place the stainless bowl on top of pot to create a double boiler. Lower heat and cook mixture while whisking

constantly. As the mixture cooks, it will thicken and air will be incorporated. Continue to cook, while whisking, until mixture has an airy, mousse-like consistency. Whisk butter cubes in, one at a time, until they have been fully incorporated. Add salt. Remove from heat and whisk over an ice bath to chill. Reserve.

SHORT RIB:
4   ounces wagyu-style beef short rib
Kosher salt
Freshly ground black pepper
1   tablespoon butter
1   tablespoon tamari

Season short rib with salt and black pepper; place the seasoned meat on hottest part of grill to get a nice sear on the meat. Cook on one side until meat has a good crust on it, flip over, and move to a less hot spot of the grill. Once flipped, baste melted butter and tamari on meat repeatedly. Continue to cook meat until desired doneness: We prefer medium rare. Remove from grill and let rest for 4 to 5 minutes to allow juice to circulate back into meat.

Place a large spoonful of beer curd on plate, and drag the end of a spoon across curd in a fluid motion. Place sliced peaches on the plate in random intervals around the beer curd. Slice rested meat in about six thin slices. Place in two clusters, slices intact, on top of the curd and next to a few peaches. Place grilled onions next to the peaches and sliced meat, about five rings per plate. Finish the plate with some ground juniper to fill some of the blank space. Serve immediately. Serves 1.

lake austin spa resort

▼▼▼▼▼▼▼▼▼▼▼▼▼▼▼▼▼▼▼▼▼▼▼▼▼▼▼▼▼▼▼▼

TERRY CONLAN HAS TRAVELED A LONG ROAD TO HIS IDYLLIC SETTING on the banks of blue-green Lake Austin, where much of the year his cooking and serving are serenaded by engine growls and the excited shouts of water skiers, wake boarders, and other thrill-seekers trying to be Matthew McConaughey. Yet even though he cooks every day and night in a spa, and even though he counts calories and fat grams with the best of them, the one road he's never wanted to travel is the one leading to "spa cuisine."

At least that's true as long as we define "spa cuisine" the way he does, as a progression of dishes based more on deprivation than flavor, with fake ingredients most often subbing for real and with the numbers underneath the name counting for more than any pleasure delivered to the palate. Terry, after all, is a Texas chef, from this vast land in which "chicken-frying" anything is an open invitation to pour on the cream gravy. He enjoys such no-holds-barred eating experiences, and he knows that most of the guests he feeds three meals a day enjoy them, too. All he wants is to discover better ways of getting us there.

"I was never interested in producing diet food," Terry says, pronouncing the words slowly and carefully as the dogma they've become at Lake Austin Spa. "I wasn't interested in producing food that people ate just because they had to. What I want, every day, is to produce food that people say: I can't *believe* this is healthy. We chefs take our creative side and we just start working within the rules."

What Terry calls "the rules" might sound simple enough. But within them you can identify most of the trends that have changed the American culinary landscape over the past two or three decades. At their most basic, the rules point any cook toward replacing high-fat cooking methods—yes, like "chicken-frying"—with low-fat methods like baking, roasting, grilling, and smoking. (As an aside, Terry insists that traditional Texas BBQ is low fat, since "low and slow" wood-smoking adds not a single gram of fat.) With that swap firmly in place, the goal quickly becomes achieving the flavor and texture people want when they order fried foods, but without all that oil. And that's where the rest of Terry's "rules" start fitting in.

The pursuit of great flavor without much added fat has been aided mightily by the culinary community's broad embrace of better products. Nothing, Terry says, could ever be healthier than the modern chef's approach of spending a bit more on fresh, locally grown, seasonal, and organic meats, seafoods, and produce—and then trying not to mess them up too much in the kitchen. Oil in Terry's world tends to be extra-virgin olive, and even with that, the dramatic flavors most often come from herb-infused vinegars, spry citrus concoctions, and other good-for-you pamperings that stand on their own without any kind of calorie counting. Such things might strike the uninitiated as unlikely to replace cream and butter in the typical cook's arsenal, but they do so with terrific results at Lake Austin Spa.

And finally, since flavor is the goal of all good cooking, Terry finds himself increasingly drawn to cuisines long undervalued by European chefs, as well as by their old-time American brethren trained in *cuisine classique*.

Asian tastes, for instance, are bright and powerful, not to mention increasingly appreciated by a wide audience in this country, as are the flavor profiles of the Mediterranean and Latin America. You don't even have to live without Tex-Mex cheese enchiladas at Lake Austin Spa, thanks to Terry's tireless pursuit of what he knows his guests won't believe they can actually have for lunch or dinner.

"I go for color, crunch, and contrast," Terry says. "If I get all three of 'em in one dish, then I'm onto something. And you know, I like to tell folks it was actually Columbus who discovered spa cuisine. The foods he ate in the Americas were completely organic, completely local, completely seasonal, and completely sustainable. If that ain't spa cuisine, I don't know what is." He ponders the many ironies of his nearly 20 years at Lake Austin Spa, then brightens into an impish grin. "I'm known as being one of the best spa chefs in America. But to me that's like being one of the best baseball players in Russia."

Some who've been guests at the all-inclusive resort might argue that Terry "not knowing" what spa cuisine is, well, is the very best thing about his food. The chef admits he has little interest in seeing or tasting what other spas around the country or the world are doing. When he and his wife travel, they invariably opt for long road trips built around checkpoints that include the best restaurants a diner can visit. They've even been known to rework a route, whether in the Pacific Northwest or Tuscany, just because the place they want to eat is closed for vacation that week. As anyone who travels on his or her stomach will tell you, the world's most famous restaurants are serving anything but spa cuisine.

Most importantly, Terry's no-compromise pursuit of flavor within the canon of healthy dining comes from the fact that his upbringing started him out as a full-bore Texas eater, and only then trained him as a full-bore Texas chef. Growing up in Dallas, Terry first knew only his mother's cooking, which he remembers as good, filling, and largely unexciting. "It was the mid to late '60s," he offers, "and food was just fuel." The epiphany came later, at UT in Austin, when Terry started cooking for a succession of college friends and roommates. He quickly became the guy in any group who went to buy the groceries, then raced home to look up what he'd bought in a growing collection of cookbooks. Of course, in those days, there weren't all that many cookbooks to collect.

A liberal arts guy from start to finish—a double major in English and theater, no less—Terry slowly began to reconsider his employment options against the backdrop of what he was doing to pay his way. Like many his age, he found his way into

"I go for color, crunch, and contrast," Terry says. "If I get all three of 'em in one dish, then I'm onto something."

"What I want, every day, is to produce food that people say: I can't *believe* this is healthy."

restaurant work, one of the greatest and most intriguing culture clashes America has ever known. In kitchen after kitchen, every single day, soft-handed "college boys" find themselves sweating alongside scarred and usually foul-mouthed veterans who show them the way the world works. For many, Terry included, the world outside these hot, high-pressure kitchens quickly loses its allure. You never want to do anything else. You never want to *be* anything else.

"I worked in a barbecue joint, and of course I flipped a few burgers," Terry says of those now-golden days, Austin in the '60s and '70s. "I worked for one guy who ran a hippie out the door with a pair of garden shears. And I apprenticed under a 72-year-old black line cook for a woman who'd been the official housekeeper for LBJ. The entire year I spent with that old guy, he never *could* figure out what a college-educated white kid was doing working in a kitchen. He was a good guy, though, and he taught me a lot."

Not a lot of spa cuisine, we'll wager.

Over several years at a popular Austin lunch spot, Terry got his first taste of being the guy in charge, though his initiation into management was anything but voluntary. Each time a head chef ran screaming out of the kitchen, the owner quickly offered Terry the job. And he, just as quickly, suggested a friend he considered more qualified. Eventually, though, Terry ran out of friends.

"We had a set menu plus an a la carte," he recalls of those six or seven years. "All it really had to be, I was told, was 'vaguely European.' I was like a teacher who was three weeks ahead of the class. I checked out every cookbook from the Austin Public Library."

The years rolled by for Terry, with each step and each stop making him more of a professional. He returned to his alma mater (which he left nine hours short of graduation) as food manager for three years, developing UT's first-ever table-seated restaurant. And he hooked up with the partners who later gave the world Jeffrey's, mastering the flavors of Mexico and the Caribbean.

As with most chefs, though, particularly those with the values and options that come with college study, Terry felt his life changing in ways that implied his job might have to change as well. By this point, he and his wife had two sons in grade school, and the long hours associated with being a chef serving lunch and dinner had

The position at Lake Austin Spa turned out, for a chef with a family and a diverse range of experiences, to be the best of all possible worlds.

seriously lost their glimmer. "So I went into retail and got to be the soccer coach," he says. "But you know, every Sunday I looked in the newspaper for a way to get back into this business."

The position at Lake Austin Spa turned out, for a chef with a family and a diverse range of experiences, to be the best of all possible worlds.

Ever since the day he started with two and a half fulltime cooks (now he has eight), Terry has enjoyed incredible support from the resort's ownership. Initially, it was just that guests liked his food, and that was enough. When new owners came in and spent years expensively renovating the resort for a more sophisticated slice of the market, they found in Terry a disciplined and charismatic ally who could create healthy foods that would be an additional draw.

Today, explains Terry, guests stay at Lake Austin Spa between four and seven days—almost no one stays less or more. So he has placed his three menus a day on a seven-day rotation, so no guest looks at the same menu twice. At dinner, there's a choice of two appetizers, including one vegetarian, and then six entrees, again one vegetarian. As a final kiss-off to any notion of deprivation, there are always three desserts: one citrus, one chocolate, and one other sweet that reflects whatever the pastry cooks are thinking.

Lunch is a bit different, with a left side of favorites that change only twice a year, following the seasons and hopefully the temperatures as spring-summer and fall-winter. On the right side of the menu there are four specials; creating them is the daily playground of Terry and his cooks. In the summer there's always a cold fruit soup, something many guests have never sampled before, which often becomes a favorite dish of their stay.

As a guy who's mastered the oxymoron of being a "Texas healthy chef"—roughly equivalent to being a dog that walks upright on its hind legs—Terry now finds himself in demand as a culinary teacher and motivator to all who wish to change their eating, on the road to changing their lives. He teaches cooking classes regularly at the spa, especially during the weeklong Culinary Experience programs that begin on the second Sunday of each month, and he proudly reports that he has taught more classes at the Lone Star State's renowned Central Market than anybody else. He publishes recipes often in national magazines and has gathered some of his best into two cookbooks, *Lean Star Cuisine* and, his first work in hardcover, *FRESH: Healthy Cooking and Living from Lake Austin Spa Resort*.

"I never look at cooking from a clinical point of view," he reports, wiping the countertop and putting away the pans after another class at the spa. "Essentially we try to feed you *less of more*." He laughs, pleased that so many decades in professional kitchens can be summarized so quickly and cleverly. "And you know, everything has changed in the years I've been doing this. My guys now are all food people to the core. And I'm the only guy in my kitchen who doesn't have a culinary degree."

EGGPLANT FRITTERS WITH SWEET RED PEPPER TZATZIKI

FRITTERS:

1 eggplant
1 egg
1 egg white
2 teaspoons baking powder
¼ cup flour
¼ teaspoon salt
Pinch of cayenne
Grapeseed oil

Prick the eggplant several times with a fork. Grill or broil until softened and charred, turning occasionally. Split to cool and then scoop out the flesh including a little of the charred skin. Drain in a colander then blot with paper towels. Combine with the remaining ingredients in a food processor. Heat a couple of inches of oil in a sauce pan to 360° F. Dollop spoonfuls of the eggplant mixture into the oil and fry until browned and crisp. Drain on paper towels. Serve hot with the tzatziki (see recipe). Serves 4 to 6.

TZATZIKI:

1 small red bell pepper, roasted, peeled, and seeded
1½ cups plain low-fat yogurt, drained in a fine-mesh strainer for 30 minutes
½ teaspoon ground cumin
2 cloves garlic, minced
Pinch of salt
Scant pinch of cayenne
1½ teaspoons lemon juice
1½ teaspoons olive oil

Puree all. Chill.

1   cup skinned, sliced peaches, fresh or frozen
½   cup sliced nectarines
½   cup sliced plums
1   cup peeled, seeded, and chunked cucumbers
¼   cup chopped onion
¼   cup peeled, seeded, and chopped roasted
    red bell pepper
¼   cup peeled, seeded, and chopped roasted
    yellow bell pepper
2   tablespoons sugar
2   tablespoons champagne vinegar
1   tablespoon chopped mint
½   teaspoon salt
1 ½ cups peach nectar
1   tablespoon olive oil
Tabasco sauce to taste

Puree fruits, vegetables, sugar, and vinegar. Thin
as needed with nectar. Add oil. Correct seasoning.
Serve chilled. Serves 6.

BASS:
½ cup walnuts
½ teaspoon chopped rosemary
½ teaspoon chopped lemon thyme
2 cloves garlic, minced

4 (4-ounce) striped bass fillets
Salt and pepper
¼ cup Dijon mustard
1 tablespoon brandy

Preheat the oven to 400° F.

Grind the first four ingredients together in a food processor to a coarse paste. Season the fish with salt and pepper.

Whisk the mustard and brandy together, then slather onto the flesh side of the fillets. Pat on the walnut mixture. Transfer the fish, walnut side up, to a baking sheet coated with nonstick spray. Bake fish for 6 to 8 minutes.

CONFIT:
1 lemon
2 tablespoons sugar

1 tablespoon limoncello
2 tablespoons water

Cut the peel from the lemon with a knife. Julienne into thin strips. Blanch for 1 minute in boiling water. Drain and repeat two more times, refreshing the water each time. Combine the juice from the lemon with the remaining ingredients in a non-reactive sauce pan. Add the julienned peel, and simmer for 5 to 6 minutes. Cool.

CHICKPEA CAKES:
½ cup dried chickpeas
2 tablespoons chopped onion
1 clove garlic, minced
1 tablespoon chopped cilantro
8 small, pitted green olives
¼ teaspoon salt

A few grains of cayenne
¼ teaspoon baking powder
¼ cup cornmeal
1½ tablespoons flour
Olive oil

Bring the chickpeas to a boil for 10 minutes in water to cover. Turn off the heat, put a lid on the pot, and let sit for 20 minutes. Drain, and grind with the onion, garlic, cilantro, olives, salt, and cayenne. Transfer to a bowl and work in the baking powder, cornmeal, and flour. Add water as needed to achieve a moldable consistency. Shape into four ½-inch-thick discs. Sauté chickpea cakes in olive oil until browned and crisped.

Divide the cakes onto four plates, top each with a fish fillet, and spoon some confit over each. Serves 4.

MINT, AND BALSAMIC SYRUP

¼   cup balsamic vinegar
2   teaspoons red wine vinegar
2   tablespoons extra-virgin olive oil
¼   teaspoon salt
Freshly ground black pepper
1   tablespoon basil, slivered
1   tablespoon mint, slivered
3   cups cubed seedless watermelon
3   cups cubed heirloom tomatoes
¾   cup small fresh mozzarella balls
Microgreens

Reduce the balsamic vinegar by 40 percent in a non-reactive sauce pan. Cool. Combine red wine vinegar, olive oil, salt, and pepper. Toss with herbs, watermelon, tomatoes, and mozzarella. Divide onto four plates. Drizzle with a little balsamic syrup. Top each with a pinch of microgreens. Serves 4.

2 pounds grass-fed lamb (shoulder roast), trimmed and cubed
Olive oil
1 ounce pancetta, minced
1 cup diced onion
½ cup diced carrot
2 cloves garlic
Salt and pepper
1 teaspoon crushed fennel seed
1 teaspoon oregano
1 bay leaf
1 cup San Marzano tomatoes (crushed) and juice
½ cup white wine
½ cup 2% milk
6 cups cooked whole-wheat capellini pasta
½ cup freshly grated Parmesan cheese
Chopped parsley

Preheat the oven to 350° F.

Season the lamb and then brown in the oil in a heavy skillet, about 8 to 10 minutes. Set aside. Add the pancetta and a little more oil to the pan. Add the onion and carrot. Sauté until soft. Add the garlic, seasonings, tomatoes, wine, and lamb. Bring to a simmer. Cover tightly and braise for 4 hours. Uncover, add the milk, and cook until mostly evaporated. Correct seasoning. Serve with pasta, topped with cheese and parsley. Serves 6 to 8.

il sogno

il sogno

▼▼▼▼▼▼▼▼▼▼▼▼▼▼▼

THE BIGGEST SAN ANTONIO RESTAURANT NEWS OF 2009 was born not at some negotiating table, not at some contract signing, and not even at some champagne toast to future success. It was born in the moment that chef Andrew Weissman of Le Reve stood gazing at a photo from his young son's Jewish day school and realized he had been the only father unable to attend father-and-son day.

"That just broke my heart," Andrew says of his decision to shutter the nationally acclaimed French eatery after more than 11 years. The closing, he vowed, would let him concentrate his energies on being a father to his son and daughter while launching several new food and drink concepts that wouldn't require his presence 24/7. "Most of the chefs I've known, going back to when I cooked in France, were either divorced or in the process of getting a divorce. I just said, 'That's not going to be me.'"

San Antonio took the Le Reve news hard, and for weeks the newspapers, magazines, and of course the Internet were filled with tributes to a restaurant many observers hadn't thought the Tex-Mex capital of God's creation would ever sustain in the first place. For his part, Weissman viewed his decision—even on a strictly business level—as cause for neither celebration nor mourning. It was simply an idea whose time had come.

"Le Reve was just this space in time," he offers philosophically over an espresso at his new Italian restaurant Il Sogno Osteria in the Pearl Brewery development. "And it always will be what it was." As some have been multilingual enough to notice, the song for Weissman remains the same. And so does the dream. That's what Le Reve means in French, and that's what Il Sogno means in Italian. Though he studied journalism, radio, TV, and film at the University of New Mexico before earning his degree in that concentration at the University of North Texas, he now says opening a restaurant was his big dream all along. And to accomplish what he did at Le Reve required some combination of skill, intuition, and luck that he hopes will remain with him. If he achieves his *new* dream of creating and launching as many as eight new concepts, most or all at the Pearl project rising along a newly developed stretch of the San Antonio River, he'll need substantial helpings of all three qualities.

"I will still be cooking at any one of these restaurants," he says, reassuring anyone who might be silly enough to ever picture him retired. "I want people to know I'm working as hard as possible to give them a great dining experience. What I'm hoping is that I can pass on some of my philosophies to some of the guys under me. That's what this business is all about, passing on the torch of knowledge."

Andrew's handling of the Le Reve decision struck many as intensely contemporary and intensely American—buying himself more time to spend with his family by creating a larger and essentially more organized corporate structure. Yet his vision of passing on culinary knowledge was nothing less than a vision of the place he'd learned it—France. And through his own hard work and undeniable ambition to excel, Andrew was able to learn it from some of the best.

"I want people to know I'm working as hard as possible to give them a great dining experience."

Growing up in a Jewish family in San Antonio, the young chef-to-be came to see food as much at the center of life as anyone growing up in the Hispanic culture that surrounded him. His father worked a lot (too much, insists Andrew), so his mother served as the family's heart, and making good meals was one of the ways she kept it beating. Still, the link between cooking for a family and cooking for a living required Andrew to study something completely different and pursue a completely different dream.

After graduation, rather than follow his peers into the usual array of entry-level journalism jobs at newspapers and radio and television stations, Andrew traveled to Mexico City and set himself up, video camera in hand, as a freelance reporter and producer. This meant finding stories to report; shooting, writing, and editing them; and then selling his handiwork to stations back in the United States. The good news: there was more than enough news happening in Mexico in the early 1990s. The bad news, as Andrew now seriously oversimplifies: he wasn't very good.

When he wasn't trying to hawk news segments, though, he was fixing meals for the regular reporters, camera crews, and sometimes even superstars of NBC News, following major stories in and out of the network's headquarters in the posh neighborhood known as Palanca. "George Lewis of NBC came to me and said it was some of the best food he'd ever had," recalls Andrew. "I remember lying awake in bed that night. The next day I said, You know, I'm not very good at this. So I came back, went to the CIA, and worked my tail off."

At the Culinary Institute of America in Hyde Park, New York, you get the picture of that same drive Andrew had applied to TV journalism suddenly aimed full bore at the act of making dinner. And even his difficult classwork Monday through Friday wasn't enough, so Andrew drove into Manhattan every weekend to work in the kitchen of a French master chef. It was more this experience than even his excellence at the CIA that got him invited to France for a year of what chefs call *stages*.

Working every station, absorbing every skill, Andrew took these lessons to heart. He was also, of course, building his resume in classic French cuisine, something that might be a good idea for a Jewish kid from San Antonio. He cooked at the Restaurant

He cooked at the Restaurant Bernard Andrieux, at the Hotel de la Poste, and, most impressively, at the legendary Restaurant Troisgros in Roanne.

Bernard Andrieux, at the Hotel de la Poste, and, most impressively, at the legendary Restaurant Troisgros in Roanne.

Andrew was lured back to the States by the opening of Le Cirque 2000 in New York City, a high-profile modernization of one of the Big Apple's most revered restaurants. "We had Chuck Mangione in the kitchen one night, playing for us while we cooked," he remembers with a grin. Still, within a few months of coming onboard as Le Cirque's saucier, some of the place's veterans started poking around to get their old jobs back, and the kid from Texas was the newest hire. Andrew let himself be lured away by another New York French place, this one called Chez Gertrude, but his head and heart were already turning toward home.

"I was cooking all the food, and the chefs weren't even cooking," Andrew says. "So I thought, Man, I could do this on my own."

As it turned out, amazingly enough, he could. During a brief family visit to San Antonio, his sister showed him a tiny vacant space in a downtown building and within a few moments of looking at it, Andrew had a plan. He scraped together the rather modest investment required to open the doors—$63,000, he recalls—and, in honor of the spot this venture came to occupy in his still-young life, he turned to French and called it simply The Dream.

There were naysayers, of course, people who insisted no one in San Antonio—not local and not tourist—would pay *this much* for dinner, would plan ahead enough to make reservations, or would slip into a jacket when it's 103 degrees outside in the summer. The success Le Reve enjoyed almost from Day One is testament not only to Andrew's faith in old San Antonio but also to his intuition about its present and its future.

"There's a lot of people here who do great Mexican food," he laughs. "And I'm not one of them. I wanted to plant my flag in my hometown, to be surrounded by family and friends. In some ways, I guess, my ignorance was my bliss. But now we're opening things in San Antonio—businesses, opportunities of all kinds—that are starting to attract the creative class. We're starting to see that influx of individuals who see that the quality of life here is amazing. The demand is there, and the entrepreneurial spirit will rise to the occasion."

Though you get the impression Andrew could never be without "entrepreneurial spirit" for long, his own has been rammed into warp speed by hooking up with the guys behind the born-again Pearl Brewery, which promises to be the biggest shot in the arm to San Antonio since 1964 when the Hemisfair left the Riverwalk and the city's entire tourism industry in its wake.

Building from the graceful brick remains of the old brewery, local developer Kit Goldsbury and his partners have created the first home for the Culinary Institute of America outside New York and Napa (with a distinct commitment to promoting Latin flavors and developing Hispanic restaurant professionals) and are now steaming full-speed toward a dining, shopping, and entertainment destination. If any further proof were needed, beyond the sounds of construction and the steel beams crisscrossing the blue autumn sky, there is the fact that the Riverwalk has been *extended* to reach the Pearl Brewery.

"I was cooking all the food, and the chefs weren't even cooking," Andrew says. "So I thought, Man, I could do this on my own."

Andrew's Il Sogno, not surprisingly once you get to know him, is only the first of many fresh ideas he's been tossing around. Yet for San Antonio, it has already proven itself a keeper. Serving contemporary Italian cuisine in a sleek and stylish setting, to a soundtrack that meanders from pleasantly cheesy Italian pop to the less-angry Bob Marley, this open kitchen with its wood-fired oven and its small army of chefs turns out an amazing array of antipasti, pastas, soups, and pizzas, plus some "center-of-the-plate" seafood and meat entrees as well.

Within a few months of getting Il Sogno on its feet, Andrew moved to incorporate his Sandbar seafood concept into the Pearl, moving it from its downtown location. There were advantages, since the original had no hot kitchen and had to get those items carted across underground from Le Reve. The new place has a kitchen of its own, standing ready to augment the pleasures already derivable from ice-cold oysters, clams, and other wonders associated with the East Coast.

As his restaurant empire continues to grow—all ventures so far within a two-minute walk of each other— Andrew knows what star he needs and wants to steer by, and it isn't the one somebody might hang on his dressing-room door. It's the one that glows from his Costa Rican wife, Maureen; their son, Maxwell Joaquin; and their daughter, Ella Maxim. And maybe, in ways all good, it also glows from the mother who directed his notions of self-worth early on. At the very least, Andrew chuckles, she'll always make sure her son, the famous chef, serves an acceptable cup of coffee.

"My mom could have the best meal in the world," he says, gazing intently into the espresso he made for himself and the foam-swirled cappuccino he crafted for a visitor. "But if she has a bad coffee, she's not going back."

¼ cup vegetable oil

8 (2-inch-thick) center-cut pieces of veal shank, bone in

3 cups dry white wine

3 onions, diced

3 carrots, diced

½ cup garlic cloves, peeled

1 quart chicken stock

1 (15-ounce) can San Marzano or other crushed tomatoes

1 bunch fresh sage

3 bay leaves

Salt and pepper to taste

Preheat the oven to 325° F.

In a large roasting pan, heat the oil over medium-high heat until it starts to smoke, then add the shanks until they are caramelized top and bottom. Remove the meat from the pan and deglaze with the wine, scraping up the browned bits from the bottom with a wooden spoon. Add the onion, carrot, and garlic. Return the meat to the pan. Pour in the chicken stock and enough water for the liquid to cover the bones. Add the tomatoes, sage, and bay leaves. Cover the pan with aluminum foil and cook in the oven for 4 hours, until the meat is falling off the bone.

Once meat is cooked, pour the pan juices into a separate pot and reduce by about half over high heat. Season to taste with salt and pepper. Serve each osso buco in a warmed bowl, ladling liquid and vegetables over the top. Serves 8.

1   pound asparagus
2   teaspoons unsalted butter
⅓   teaspoon Maldon salt
2   teaspoons minced chives
½   ounce black truffle, thinly sliced (optional)
1   tablespoon truffle oil
½   teaspoon freshly ground black pepper
4   eggs
2   teaspoons parsley

Prepare the asparagus by slicing off the woody bottom, and peeling and blanching for 2 minutes in boiling salted water. Shock the asparagus in ice water to stop cooking, and drain. Keep warm.

Butter four pieces of plastic wrap. Sprinkle plastic wrap with sea salt, cut chives, black truffle, truffle oil, and ground pepper. Press "seasoned" plastic into four shallow cups and crack one egg into each plastic bowl. Tie off the packages. Poach eggs in simmering water about 4 minutes. Unwrap package and place egg on top of cooked asparagus. Garnish with parsley. Serves 4.

¼ cup vegetable oil

12 to 15 pounds raw lobster shells

1 pound onion, thinly sliced

½   pound carrot, thinly sliced

½ pound celery, thinly sliced

¼ cup tomato paste

½ cup plus 1 splash cognac or brandy

2 tablespoons finely chopped shallots

1 pound clams in shell

½ pound mussels in shell, beard removed

1 pound raw shrimp, peeled and deveined

8 (5-ounce) pieces fresh cod or other mild, white-fleshed fish, skin off

⅓ cup all-purpose flour

Salt and pepper

Preheat the oven to 350° F.

Heat about half the oil in a large roasting pan over medium-high heat until it's almost smoking, then add the lobster shells and roast in the oven, stirring regularly, until aromatic and bright red, about 20 minutes. Bash the shells with a mallet to release all liquid, forming a browned "fond" at the bottom on the pan. Over medium heat, add the "mirepoix" of onion, carrot, and celery, stirring with a wooden spoon until the vegetables start to caramelize. Then add the tomato paste and stir, scraping bits from the bottom of the pan. Deglaze with the brandy and scrape some more. Add enough water to cover the shells immediately.

Simmer for about 2 hours; do not boil or the stock will be cloudy. Strain through a chinois or other fine-mesh strainer.

To cook the shellfish, ladle some of this stock into a hot, dry pan until the level reaches about half an inch. Add the shallots. Add the clams and cover the pan to create steam. After about 1 or 2 minutes, add the mussels and shrimp, covering them for about 2 minutes more.

Meanwhile, dredge the fish in the flour, knocking off all excess. Season with salt and pepper. Heat the rest of the vegetable oil in an oven-proof pan over medium heat. When hot, color all the fish pieces on the presentation side first, then flip them over and set the pan in the oven to finish cooking until firm, only about 5 minutes. To serve, combine liquid from the shellfish with the remaining stock. Add a splash of cognac or brandy. Season with salt and pepper, then strain the hot broth into a pitcher. Place a mixture of shellfish in the bottom of eight warmed bowls and set fish atop the shellfish. Pour the hot soup around the seafood at the table. Serves 8.

LOBSTER RAVIOLI WITH SAFFRON SAUCE

1   quart lobster stock (see cod recipe, page 190)
1   pinch saffron threads
2   cups heavy cream
Salt and pepper to taste
5   (1 ¼- to 1 ½-pound) lobsters, steamed
¾   pound raw shrimp, peeled and deveined
¼   cup minced onion
2   tablespoons minced chives
Juice of 1 lemon
1   pound fresh sheet pasta
1   egg, beaten

Pour the lobster stock into a pot and reduce it by half over high heat. During the reduction, add the saffron threads for color and flavor. When liquid is reduced, add the cream and reduce until thickened and velvety. Season to taste with salt and pepper. Remove the lobster meat from the shells and cut into bite-sized pieces.

To prepare the filling, combine all but about a half pound of lobster with the shrimp, onion, chives, salt, pepper, and lemon juice. Run the mixture through a food processor until it's smooth. Spread the pasta sheets onto a clean, dry surface, and spoon the filling in small mounds with enough space in between each mound for a finger. Fill the bottom row this way, then fold the top over until it covers the mounds and lines up with the bottom edge of the pasta. Press down in between the mounds with your finger, forming the ravioli. Spread the edges with beaten egg before crimping. Cut them apart using a knife.

Cook the ravioli for 3 to 4 minutes in boiling salted water, then remove with a slotted spoon. Add the remaining chunks of lobster to the sauce and heat, then ladle the liquid into warmed bowls along with about five ravioli per person. Garnish with the lobster meat from the sauce. Serves 8.

5   ounces unsalted butter
⅓   cup sugar
1   pinch salt
3   eggs
1½ to 2 cups all-purpose flour
10   ounces (62% cacao) chocolate, such as Valrhona
7   ounces unsalted butter
6   egg yolks
¼   cup sugar
About 1 cup Nutella spread

To make the tart shells (with enough for a pie crust left over), combine the butter, sugar, and salt in a food processor. While processing, crack one egg into the mixture and let it incorporate. Dump in 1 ½ cups of flour, adding more in small amounts if the mixture is too wet. Remove the formed ball from the processor and wrap in plastic wrap. Refrigerate for at least 1 hour.

Unwrap the dough and roll out in eight small sections as thin as you can, preferably ¹⁄₁₆ to ⅛ inch. Press these thin sections into a 3-inch-wide tart shell and set all these on a sheet pan. Set in the freezer to "set up," at least 20 minutes.

Preheat the oven to 350° F.

Bake the empty tart shells until golden brown, about 8 to 10 minutes.

Prepare the filling by melting the chocolate with the butter atop a double boiler. In a bowl, whisk the yolks and two whole eggs together until combined, then mix in the sugar. Remove the chocolate-butter mixture from the heat and whisk in the egg mixture.

Spoon Nutella into each baked shell, spreading it around the bottom and up the sides, making a bed for the topping. Fill the rest of the way with the filling. Return tarts to the oven until only about a dime-sized area at the center of the filling appears to be wet, about 8 minutes.

Serve tarts warm with ice cream or whipped cream— or both. Serves 8.

cochineal

▼▼▼▼▼▼▼▼▼▼▼▼▼▼▼▼

IN THE TINY BUT ARTSY WEST TEXAS TOWN OF MARFA, Illinois-born Tom Rapp and Okinawa-born Toshi Sakihara know how to measure success. It's a dining room that's full nearly every night, mostly with people they know on a first-name basis and most of whom dine here several nights a week. On New York's Upper East Side, however, where they both learned the restaurant business from the ground up, they might well measure success by the scrapbook full of mentions, announcements, and reviews they'll show to anyone who seems interested.

"We brought to New York something it wanted and couldn't get," Tom explains, turning the pages of the scrapbook about the restaurant known as Etats-Unis. "We served simple global home cooking, though we always thought of it as an American restaurant. We almost called the place Ellis Island, reflecting the American experience." He laughs quietly. "I'm glad we didn't name it that, but it was an idea."

According to Tom and Toshi, and backed up by references in New York newspapers and magazines, New Yorkers were tired of food that was overhandled, overtowered, overindulged—over *full of itself*. They wanted something that tasted like Mama used to make, except—as several reviewers asked pointedly—who has a Mama who cooks this well anymore? For New Yorkers, Etats-Unis became a home away from home, in more ways than one.

Most people with a successful restaurant on the Upper East Side, where Tom and Toshi functioned efficiently as co-chefs, don't turn into Texans overnight. But that's what happened to them, over a three-day weekend when they visited Marfa to see the contemporary art installations of the late Donald Judd. Judd had created the new artistic Marfa, beginning when he bought a ranch here in the 1970s and continuing beyond his death with the Chinati Foundation. And he certainly played a role, albeit posthumously, in attracting Marfa's two best-known chefs.

"We'd been looking to move out of New York," offers Tom. "We looked at Ojai and Santa Barbara in California, also at San Miguel de Allende in Mexico. We came here for a weekend and bought a house here."

Cochineal, named after a tiny bug from which the Spaniards made a red dye that they shipped to Europe from the seventeenth century into the nineteenth, opened in May of 2008. It had already been quite a journey, taking two and a half years to open from the day Tom and Toshi became Marfa homeowners. The building started as an old house from the 1800s but required so many repairs and upgrades that it became "a new house with some old stuff in it."

Featuring an open kitchen at which diners like to stand with their wine watching the cooking, Cochineal can seat about 40 at any one time, though when his young kitchen crew reaches its potential, Tom and Toshi hope to push that to 50. The dining room walls are dark slate gray, with red wainscoting all around and some striking white felt strips hanging from the ceiling. The tables are made of mesquite, the favored barbecue wood of West Texas, and there are no tablecloths in sight.

"We are a white-tablecloth restaurant without the fake elegance of white tablecloths," Tom explains. He thinks a moment, doing the math. "This is unlike anything within about 800 miles."

"We'd been looking to move out of New York," offers Tom.

Tom and Toshi seem comfortable with each other, as partners and as co-chefs. But that doesn't diminish the drama that led two quite different lives from Manhattan to a town of 2,121 into the kitchen in the first place. Tom started out an architect, a successful one, with a wife and kids, including a son whose love of food helped push him into the restaurant business. Toshi started out an accountant, learning his profession mostly in San Antonio after coming to America, but he ended up crunching numbers for Japanese companies in New York.

Tom's career was a triumph of American education and European culture. He grew up in Connecticut and spent years as a student, first at Brown and then at Yale for graduate work. Strewn throughout his early life, however, were epiphany-producing travel experiences that pointed him toward cooking. Serving with the U.S. Army in Korea in the late 1950s, for instance, he experienced not only exotic Korean staples like kimchee but made many forays into Japan, tasting Kobe beef, sushi, and sashimi before there was such a thing in the United States.

Tom and his wife also made the first of several visits to France during a break from grad school; people kept hiring him to stop studying architecture and actually do some. He worked for a firm in Paris and fell in love with French food, then returned to Yale just long enough to get hired away again by the dean's firm in New York. By this point, Tom was cooking at home all the time, for his wife and two children, and for any dinner party he could hustle up like a pool shark looking to run the table.

During one early trip to Paris, a search for a French cookbook in English turned up rumors of such a work on the horizon, despite the fact that, as Tom puts it, America was still eating Wonder bread back then. And while three women living in Paris were the authors of this much-anticipated book, one got mentioned a bit more than the others—someone named Julia Child.

"Believe me," Tom recalls, "between the two of us, my wife and I cooked our way through that whole book. By the time you do that, it's an education. We did a lot of dinner parties, and my son Jonathan ate it up. Food was very central to our house. I gave Jonathan a bottle of Chateau Yquem (the world's most famous sauternes) on his 13th birthday in 1967. We all drank it, but he was in control of it." Tom smiles. "I approved."

Many years later, after Tom and Toshi had met and begun their partnership in the kitchen and beyond, cookbooks remained an essential part of their lives. In the early days of Etats-Unis, opened with Jonathan, diners couldn't help noticing the shelf near the entrance, laden with cookbooks from around the world. There is such a shelf as well at Cochineal in Marfa, its promises of French, Italian, Vietnamese, or Latin American flavors made real on a menu that changes virtually every night.

Tom's career was a triumph of American education and European culture.

For his part, even as Tom was gravitating toward the savory side of cooking, Toshi was gravitating, somewhat miraculously, toward the sweet. Japan has no baking tradition, he explains, meaning that as far back as his beginnings in Okinawa, he was fascinated by what an oven could do. This interest continued when he came to the United States as a student in 1980, first studying English and then moving into accounting. Though Okinawa seems a long way from San Antonio, Toshi insists that his home island has so many American Army bases that he was comfortable with Americans as far back as he can remember.

"In San Antonio, I baked the same thing over and over until it was perfect, and then I moved on," Toshi recalls. "I made muffins, pecan pies, everything. It was a kind of self-apprenticeship."

"Can you imagine," Tom cuts in, smiling with obvious affection, "an accountant doing the same recipe over and over, until it's perfect?"

Tom and Toshi met socially and lived together from 1990 onward. When Toshi was let go by his New York accounting firm, he took over desserts and all other baking at Etats-Unis. Tom, naturally, was delighted to see at least one task lifted off his shoulders. All told, Etats-Unis operated from 1992 until its sale in 2005, the first eight years in partnership with Jonathan, who eventually left to run a restaurant of his own in Connecticut.

On this particular night, the one-page typed menu offers a white and a red wine by the glass, followed by five appetizers, an equal number of entrees, and four of Toshi's desserts. Two of the most popular starters (with variations appearing on many, if not most, nights) are the potato gnocchi with some combination of shredded Brussels sprouts and zucchini in a sauce of Parmesan and pinenuts, and the English cheddar cheese soufflé with yet another bubbly-hot Parmesan sauce.

Among the entrees, what's old seems new again—and what seems familiar slightly, delightfully askew. Rack of lamb not only gets grilled over West Texas mesquite but gets paired with fresh mint butter, baby greens, and a terrine of, you guessed it, English cheddar and potato. Duck turns up as crispy-skinned confit atop sautéed spinach with golden raisins and garlic-happy cannellini beans. Japan gets a dramatic nod in the seared sushi-grade marlin, perched in all its rare beauty on sushi rice with soy, wasabi, and Japanese pickles. For dessert, most tables get at least one chocolate soufflé, but it's hard to talk Regulars into any sweet other than Toshi's date pudding with warm rum–caramel sauce.

Today at Cochineal, Tom and Toshi seem happy with the many difficult choices they've made—not the least of which was opening an ambitious

Diners couldn't help noticing the shelf near the entrance, laden with cookbooks from around the world.

fine-dining restaurant in Marfa. Sure, good wines were hard to come by in the beginning. And sure, whenever they call someone to chat, they're probably in the car going to or from El Paso (three hours each way) on a food run. But little by little, a distribution network is being cobbled together. Maybe more things will come to them eventually, rather than vice versa.

As they glance around the dining room on another busy night, they see a lot more than their restaurant turning a profit. They see friends they embraced from their arrival in Marfa the only way they knew how—by cooking for them. And if all the best things we do in life are for some combination of love and money, it's not hard to understand that, first and foremost at this stage of their life together, this place was never about the money.

"When we moved here, we started doing dinner parties several times a week," Tom says, and Toshi smiles his appreciation of the memory. "You move here and you know everybody in no time. By the end of three years, we had fed most of the people you see here in this restaurant tonight. They knew us and liked what we were doing. We wanted to be part of the community, not just a restaurant that's selling food."

"We wanted to be part of the community, not just a restaurant that's selling food."

VEAL CHEEKS:

8 veal cheeks, lightly trimmed
  (no need to remove any silver skin)
Olive oil
4 cups mirepoix (diced carrot, onion, and celery)
1 cup white wine
1 quart chicken stock
1 tablespoon herbes de Provence,
  or other fresh herbs
Salt and freshly ground black pepper to taste

HORSERADISH MASHED POTATOES:

6 Idaho baking potatoes
¾ to 1 cup milk, heated to simmer
6 tablespoons melted butter
¼ cup (or to taste) freshly grated horseradish
Salt and freshly ground black pepper to taste

Preheat the oven to 350° F.

Place the veal cheeks, silver skin side down, in a pan covered with olive oil, being careful not to crowd. Brown on both sides over medium heat, in batches if necessary. Spread mirepoix over the bottom of a baking dish large enough to hold the cheeks and press cheeks down into the mirepoix. In a bowl, combine the wine, stock, and herbs, then pour over the veal cheeks. Cover the pan tightly with foil and braise in the oven for 3 hours. Uncover and bake for an additional 30 minutes, adding stock as needed to keep the cheeks covered. Remove the cheeks, cover, and keep them warm. Strain the liquid from the pan and keep that warm too, seasoning if necessary.

To prepare the mashed potatoes, raise the oven temperature to 450° F. Wash the potatoes and bake them for 45 minutes. Cool enough to handle, then cut them in two and force them through a ricer into a large bowl. Discard skins. Whip in the hot milk, melted butter, and horseradish in stages. Season to taste with salt and pepper. Add more milk if a creamier consistency is preferred. Top with a little extra butter.

Spoon mashed potatoes onto warmed dinner plates and top each with a veal cheek and sauce. Serves 8.

SHROPSHIRE BLEU CHEESE SOUFFLED PUDDINGS

½   cup butter
½   cup flour
2   cups half-and-half
½   cup Shropshire or other high-quality bleu cheese
    (about ¼ pound)
¼   cup grated Parmesan, plus extra for garnish
8   egg yolks
Salt and freshly ground black pepper to taste
10 egg whites, room temperature
1   pinch cream of tartar
½   cup heavy cream
Chopped fresh chives

Preheat the oven to 350° F.

Melt the butter in a sauce pan over low heat. Add the
flour, stirring until completely incorporated. Slowly stir in half-and-half. Cook and stir mixture for 2 minutes, or
until thickened and smooth. Stir in cheeses and heat until melted. Remove pan from heat and beat in egg yolks
one at a time. Season with salt and pepper to taste. The mixture should be slightly over-seasoned.

In a bowl, beat the egg whites with the cream of tartar and the cream, using an electric mixer, until soft peaks
form. Do not overbeat. Carefully fold the egg whites into the cheese mixture. Divide butter into eight buttered
4-by-2½-inch round ramekins, filling to about ¼ inch from the rim. Carefully place the filled ramekins into a
shallow roasting pan and pour in enough hot water to reach about a third of the way up their sides. Bake until
the tops are set and brown, 40 to 45 minutes. Remove from the oven. Serve hot in ramekins, garnished with
Parmesan and chives. Serves 8.

GNOCCHI:
1 ½ pounds Idaho potatoes
⅞ cup unbleached all-purpose flour
2 tablespoons kosher salt
¼ pound butter
Pepper to taste

SAUCE:
8 large Brussels sprouts
½ cup pine nuts
1 large clove garlic
1 tablespoon olive oil
½ pound butter
⅓ cup water
8 drops truffle oil
1 tablespoon finely chopped chives
Salt and freshly ground black pepper to taste

Preheat the oven to 450° F.

To prepare the gnocchi, wash the potatoes and bake for 45 minutes. Let cool enough to handle, then cut in half and force through a ricer into a large bowl, discarding the skins. Add flour along with salt and pepper, and toss (not stir) until mixed. Melt the butter and add to the mixture. Knead thoroughly until combined. Form individual gnocchi by rolling ½-ounce portions between the palms to form smooth balls. Gently press each one between the thumb and the tines of a dinner fork to create a dent on one side and the tine depressions on the other.

To prepare the sauce, shred the Brussels sprouts. Gently toast the pine nuts in a dry pan until lightly golden. Mince the garlic, and toast in olive oil only until soft and lightly colored. Combine the Brussels sprouts and butter in a large sauté pan, gently cooking until soft. Add the pine nuts, toasted garlic, and water, stirring to combine. Season to taste with salt and pepper.

Cook gnocchi in a large pot of simmering salted water only until the gnocchi rise to the surface. Skim out as they rise, placing them in a wet or lightly oiled sauté pan in a single layer. Combine with the sauce and serve as quickly as possible, topped with chives and the drops of truffle oil. Serves 8.

ALMOND CAKES:

⅔   cup ground almonds
¾   cup plus 3 tablespoons sugar
3   tablespoons all-purpose flour
4   egg whites

ROASTED PEARS:

4   ripe pears
1 ½ cups dry white wine
½   cup water
¾   cup sugar
¼   cup agave nectar, divided
Zest of 1 lemon
2   tablespoons butter
⅛   teaspoon ground clove
½   teaspoon ground nutmeg
½   teaspoon ground cinnamon
½   teaspoon ground black pepper

RED WINE SAUCE:

1   cup red wine
1   cup roasting syrup (from pears)
Zest of 1 lemon
2   pieces star anise

CHOCOLATE SAUCE:

4   ounces Callebaut bittersweet chocolate
½   cup heavy cream
1   tablespoon Grand Marnier liqueur
Strawberry quarters for garnish

Preheat the oven to 350° F.

Prepare the almond cakes by mixing the almonds, ¾ cup sugar, and the flour. Whip the egg whites until soft peaks foam. Add the 3 tablespoons sugar and continue whipping. Fold the dry mix into the egg white mixture. Drop four teaspoons of this batter into eight 3 ½-inch-wide, ½-inch-tall baking rings. Bake in the oven until cooked through, 20 to 25 minutes.

Slice the pears in half lengthwise and scoop out the center with a small spoon. In a baking pan, mix the wine, water, sugar, ⅛ cup agave nectar, and lemon zest. Cook over high heat until the sugar is dissolved, and then another 2 to 3 minutes. Raise the oven temperature to 400° F. Arrange the scooped-out pears in the syrup in the baking pan, cover, and roast for 20 to 25 minutes, then turn them over and cook another 20 to 25 minutes. Remove the pears, saving the syrup. In another pan, melt the butter and sprinkle in the clove, nutmeg, cinnamon, black pepper, and remaining ⅛ cup agave nectar. Stir well and add the roasted pears, coating them well on both sides.

Make the red wine sauce by combining all ingredients in a sauce pan and cooking until thick and syrupy. Then make the chocolate sauce by combining all ingredients in a sauce pan and cooking, stirring constantly, over medium-low heat until the chocolate melts and the sauce becomes smooth.

To assemble the dessert, place an almond cake on each of eight dessert plates. Pour about 1 tablespoon of the chocolate sauce over the center of each cake, letting it spill down the sides. Arrange a pear half atop the sauce, and top with strawberry quarters. Pour about ½ tablespoon of the red wine sauce over the dessert. Serves 8.